# Thailand travel guide 2023

Enchanting Thailand: A Journey through the Land of Smiles "Unveiling the Rich Cultural Heritage, Tropical Paradises, and Unforgettable Adventures"

By

**Esther L. George**

# Table of Contents

Preface                                                                    7

Introduction                                                              11

Welcome to Thailand: Discover the Land of Smiles 11

The history of Thailand                                          14

Preparing for a journey to Thailand                    19

Visa Requirements and Practical Tips:             20

Packing Guide for a Memorable Trip:                22

My first trip to Thailand                                        23

Accommodation choices for tourists in Thailand   26

Depending on interest and budget recommended
places to stay in Thailand                                    29

Some of the Luxurious and affordable hotels in
Thailand and how to book (Bangkok,Chiang Mai,
Phuket,Koh Samui,Krabi,and Pattaya)             33

Food choices                                                        52

List of some eateries and restaurants in Thailand  54

Vegetarians and vegans choices                      57

Car rental services in Thailand                          61

Emergency services in Thailand                        62

Group tours                                                            63

Telecommunication 66

Activities for family. 69

Do's and don'ts 72

7 day itenary 75

Travel insurance 79

Saving money in Thailand 83

Bangkok 88
  Tips for Navigating Bangkok: 101

Chiang Mai 106
  Exploring the historical wonders of the Old City in Chiang Mai 109

Doi Suthep 113
  Experiencing the Charm of the Sunday Night Market 116

Phuket and the Andaman Sea 124
  Relaxing on Pristine Beaches and Island Getaways 127

Exploring Phang Nga Bay's Stunning Limestone Karsts 134
  Discovering the Cultural Gems of Old Phuket Town 138

Chiang Rai: 142

Doi Tung: 148

Mae Sai: 151

Pai: 155

Mae Hong Son: 159

Other Beyond Destinations: 162

Uncovering the Mysteries of the White Temple (Wat Rong Khun) 163

Hill Tribe Encounters and Cultural Immersion 166

Golden Triangle: Where Three Countries Converge 173

Ayutthaya 177

Sukhothai 180

Lopburi 183

Khao Sok National Park 186

Doi Inthanon 189

Erawan Falls 192

Thai massage 201

Loy Krathong and Songkran: Thailand's Colourful Festivals 205

Amphawa 208

Ko Tao 212

Trang 215

Safety tips    219

Transportation Options and Getting Around    222

Language Essentials and Useful Phrases    226

Recommended Travel Apps and Websites    229

Conclusion    232

# Preface

Welcome to "The Land of Smiles: Unveiling the Rich Cultural Heritage, Tropical Paradises, and Unforgettable Adventures." In this book, we invite you on a journey through the enchanting country of Thailand, where vibrant traditions, breathtaking landscapes, and warm hospitality come together to create an unforgettable experience.

Thailand, known as the "Land of Smiles," captivates visitors with its diverse and fascinating cultural heritage. From the majestic temples of Bangkok to the ancient ruins of Ayutthaya and the serene beauty of Chiang Mai, this country is a treasure trove of history and spirituality. We will delve into the intricate details of these architectural wonders, revealing the stories behind them and their significance in Thai society.

But Thailand is not just about its cultural heritage. It boasts some of the most breathtaking tropical paradises in the world. Picture yourself lounging on pristine white-sand beaches, surrounded by crystal-clear turquoise waters in Phuket, Krabi, or Koh Samui. Immerse yourself in the blissful tranquility of these coastal gems and let the gentle ocean breeze wash away your worries.

For those seeking adventure, Thailand has an abundance of exhilarating experiences to offer. Explore dense jungles and encounter majestic elephants in their natural habitat. Trek through lush green mountains, discovering hidden waterfalls and interacting with hill tribe communities, gaining insight into their way of life. Zip-line through the treetops, take a bamboo rafting excursion, or dive into the vibrant underwater world while snorkeling or scuba diving.

As we embark on this literary journey, we aim to capture the essence of Thailand, revealing its many facets and offering a glimpse into the heart and soul of this captivating nation. Through vivid descriptions, captivating anecdotes, and practical travel advice, we hope to inspire you to embark on your own adventure and create lasting memories in the Land of Smiles.

So, join us as we uncover the secrets of Thailand, from its bustling cities to its tranquil islands, from its ancient temples to its modern attractions. Prepare to be enthralled by the rich tapestry of cultural heritage, the allure of tropical paradises, and the thrill of unforgettable adventures that await you in the Land of Smiles. We sincerely hope that "The Land of Smiles" serves as your companion, guiding you through this remarkable country and helping you make the most of your journey. We invite you to leave a review on Amazon to share your thoughts and experiences, enabling fellow travelers to discover the magic of Thailand through your eyes.

Bon voyage and happy exploring!

Esther .L George

Review: "The Land of Smiles took me on a captivating journey through Thailand's cultural heritage, tropical paradises, and thrilling adventures. The vivid descriptions and practical travel advice made it easy to plan and enjoy an unforgettable trip. This book is a must-read for anyone seeking to discover the heart and soul of the Land of Smiles!" -

# Introduction

## Welcome to Thailand: Discover the Land of Smiles

As you step foot into the captivating kingdom of Thailand, prepare to be enchanted by a land of vibrant colors, tantalizing flavors, and warm-hearted smiles. Nestled in the heart of Southeast Asia, Thailand is a country that beckons travelers with its rich cultural heritage, breathtaking landscapes, and a sense of adventure that lingers in the air.

This introduction serves as your gateway to an extraordinary journey through the Land of Smiles. Here, ancient traditions coexist harmoniously with modern dynamism, creating a tapestry of experiences that will captivate your senses and leave a lasting impression.

Thailand's capital city, Bangkok, is a bustling metropolis where skyscrapers reach for the heavens, ornate temples stand as testaments to the past, and lively street markets buzz with energy. As you navigate the vibrant streets and labyrinthine alleyways, the city's intoxicating blend of old and new will envelop you, immersing you in a whirlwind of sights, sounds, and scents.

Beyond the urban splendor of Bangkok lies a treasure trove of natural wonders. From the pristine white-sand beaches and crystalline waters of Phuket and Krabi to the mist-shrouded mountains of Chiang Mai and the lush jungles of Khao Sok National Park, Thailand's landscapes offer a diverse playground for outdoor enthusiasts and nature lovers.

Yet, it is the people of Thailand who truly make this country special. With their infectious smiles, genuine warmth, and innate hospitality, the Thai people welcome visitors with open arms. Whether you're exploring ancient temples, haggling at a bustling market, or simply strolling through a local neighborhood, you'll find yourself immersed in a culture where kindness and a sense of "sanuk" (fun) infuse every interaction.

Throughout this travel guide, we'll take you on a journey to discover the hidden gems, cultural traditions, and breathtaking landmarks that make Thailand an unforgettable destination. From the majestic palaces and sacred temples to the mouthwatering street food and traditional festivals, each chapter will unveil a different facet of this remarkable country.

Whether you're a first-time traveler or a seasoned explorer, "Welcome to Thailand: Discover the Land of Smiles" promises to be your trusted companion, providing insider tips, practical advice, and a wealth of knowledge to ensure that your adventure through Thailand is nothing short of extraordinary.

So, prepare to be swept away by the allure of Thailand, where ancient wonders meet modern marvels, and the genuine warmth of the Thai people embraces you at every turn. Get ready to create memories that will linger in your heart long after you bid farewell to this captivating land. Welcome to Thailand – a world of smiles, wonder, and endless possibilities.

# The history of Thailand

is a tapestry woven with ancient civilizations, dynamic kingdoms, cultural exchanges, and resilience in the face of external influences. From prehistoric settlements to the present day, Thailand's history has shaped its identity and cultural heritage.

Prehistoric Era:
Thailand's earliest inhabitants can be traced back to prehistoric times, with evidence of human settlements dating back over 10,000 years. Archaeological discoveries indicate that these early communities were engaged in hunting, gathering, and later, agriculture.

Dvaravati and Srivijaya Kingdoms:
Around the 6th century CE, the Dvaravati Kingdom emerged in central Thailand, characterized by Indian cultural influences and the spread of Buddhism. The region saw the construction of impressive temples and the development of a flourishing civilization.

During the 8th to 13th centuries, the powerful Srivijaya Kingdom, based in present-day Indonesia, exerted influence over parts of southern Thailand, facilitating trade and cultural exchanges between India, China, and Southeast Asia.

Sukhothai Kingdom:
The 13th century marked the rise of the Sukhothai Kingdom, considered the first independent Thai state. King Ramkhamhaeng is revered for establishing a centralized government, promoting Theravada Buddhism, and fostering cultural and religious advancements. The Sukhothai period is often hailed as a golden age, known for its artistic

achievements and the creation of the iconic Buddha statues.

Ayutthaya Kingdom:
In the 14th century, the Ayutthaya Kingdom emerged as a dominant power in the region. The kingdom prospered through trade and established diplomatic ties with European powers. Ayutthaya became a cosmopolitan city, attracting merchants, scholars, and artisans from around the world. However, in 1767, Ayutthaya fell to the Burmese, marking the end of its glorious era.

Thonburi and Rattanakosin Periods:
Following the fall of Ayutthaya, General Taksin established the short-lived Thonburi Kingdom, centered in present-day Bangkok. Taksin's reign marked a period of recovery and consolidation.

In 1782, General Chao Phraya Chakri founded the Chakri Dynasty and established Bangkok as the new capital, ushering in the Rattanakosin Period. The Chakri Dynasty continues to reign in

Thailand to this day, making it one of the world's longest-ruling royal families.

Modern Era:
In the 19th and 20th centuries, Thailand faced increasing pressure from Western colonial powers, managing to maintain its independence, with King Chulalongkorn (Rama V) undertaking significant reforms to modernize the country. Thailand's modernization efforts continued under subsequent monarchs, embracing constitutional monarchy and fostering economic development.

Thailand faced challenges during World War II when it was occupied by Japan.
However, the post-war era saw the country's emergence as a regional economic powerhouse, with rapid industrialization and advancements in infrastructure.

Contemporary Thailand:
Thailand has experienced political transitions, social changes, and economic growth throughout

the 20th and 21st centuries. However, it has also faced periods of political instability and protests, as various factions vied for power and societal demands evolved.

Today, Thailand is a vibrant and culturally diverse nation, known for its rich heritage, picturesque landscapes, and renowned hospitality. It continues to blend tradition with modernity, welcoming visitors from around the globe to experience its unique charm and vibrant tapestry of history.

Note: The above overview provides a general summary of Thailand's history. The country's history is vast and complex, with numerous significant events and intricacies that could be explored in greater detail.

# Preparing for a journey to Thailand

Preparing for a journey to Thailand can be an exciting adventure! Here's some essential travel information, visa requirements, practical tips, and a packing guide to help you have a memorable trip.

**Essential Travel Information for Thailand:**

1. Weather: Thailand has a tropical climate with three main seasons - hot, cool, and rainy. The hot season is from March to June, the cool season from November to February, and the rainy season from July to October. Check the weather forecast before your trip to pack accordingly.

2. Currency: The official currency in Thailand is the Thai Baht (THB). It's advisable to carry some cash, but credit cards are widely accepted in tourist areas. ATMs are available throughout the country.

3. Language: The official language is Thai, but English is spoken and understood in most tourist destinations, hotels, and restaurants.

4. Safety: Thailand is generally a safe country for travelers. However, take common precautions like safeguarding your belongings, avoiding isolated areas at night, and being cautious of scams.

5. Health and Safety: Check with your healthcare provider about recommended vaccinations for Thailand. It's advisable to have travel insurance that covers medical expenses and emergency evacuation.

# Visa Requirements and Practical Tips:

1. Visa Requirements: Visitors from many countries, including the United States, European Union, Australia, and Canada, can enter

Thailand without a visa for tourism purposes for up to 30 days. However, it's essential to check the visa requirements based on your nationality before traveling. You can consult the Thai embassy or consulate in your country for up-to-date information.

2. Passport Validity: Ensure that your passport is valid for at least six months beyond your intended departure date from Thailand.

3. Visa Extensions: If you plan to stay in Thailand for more than 30 days, you can extend your visa for an additional 30 days at an immigration office in Thailand. Note that this option is only available once, and there may be a fee involved.

4. Cultural Etiquette: Thai culture values respect and politeness. It's appreciated to dress modestly, remove your shoes when entering temples or someone's home, and avoid touching people's heads, as it is considered sacred.

# Packing Guide for a Memorable Trip:

1. Clothing: Pack lightweight and breathable clothing suitable for the tropical climate. Include shorts, t-shirts, lightweight pants, a swimsuit, a hat, and a rain jacket or umbrella. For temple visits, bring a shawl or sarong to cover your shoulders.

2. Footwear: Comfortable walking shoes or sandals are a must, especially if you plan to explore cities or visit temples. Flip-flops or water shoes are handy for beach areas.

3. Travel Essentials: Don't forget to pack your passport, travel documents, travel adapters (Type A/B/C), sunscreen, insect repellent, a first aid kit, and any necessary prescription medication.

4. Electronics: Bring your smartphone, camera, charger, and any other electronic devices you

may need. A power bank is useful for keeping your devices charged on the go.

5. Other Items: Consider packing a small daypack for excursions, a travel towel, a reusable water bottle, sunglasses, a money belt or neck wallet for securing valuables, and a phrasebook or language translation app.

# My first trip to Thailand

This is a guide to your first trip to Thailand. 🇹🇭 Anyone have Thailand on their bucket list? It's time to make it happen.

Thailand is one of the most affordable countries I've visited - the flight price might be steep, but things get better when you land. 🙌

See a mini guide below for my 7-day trip, especially if it is your first time.

• Cities to cover - Bangkok (3 days) and Phuket (4 days)
• STAY: Bangkok - Valia Bangkok Hotel.
 Phuket - Amatara Resort

• Best time to visit: November to April for the best and sunniest weather ☀ However, note that it will be VERY sunny. Going in May meant it was still sunny but there were mornings of light showers. Even when it rained, it was still humid.

• Cash or card? Both! But carry cash for tipping, street food and when you go to more remote islands as ATMs are few and far between.

• Things I did?
Phuket - Day trip to Phi Phi Islands, City tour of Phuket including the Big Buddha, Visit an ethical elephant sanctuary, ATV riding and zip lining adventures.

Bangkok - Temple hop through Grand Palace, Wat Arun, Wat Pho. Do a Tuk Tuk street food tour, Go experience a floating market, Get a Thai massage. Really so much to do in Bangkok.

• General tips - Bring a scarf or two for temples. Don't book all your tours in advance - you'll find it to be more affordable when you get there. Prepare for the heat. Light and breathable fabrics ONLY. Most importantly, enjoy. But there's so much more to explore enjoy this guide and enjoy your trip.

Remember to check the weight and size restrictions of your airline to avoid any issues with your luggage.

Enjoy your trip to Thailand! It's a beautiful country with rich culture, delicious cuisine, and stunning landscapes.

# Accommodation choices for tourists in Thailand

Thailand offers a wide range of accommodation choices for tourists, catering to different preferences and budgets. Here are some popular options:

1. Hotels: Thailand has a vast selection of hotels ranging from budget-friendly options to luxury resorts. You'll find international hotel chains, boutique hotels, and local accommodations. Most major cities and tourist destinations have a variety of hotels to choose from.

2. Guesthouses: Guesthouses are smaller, more intimate accommodations often run by local owners. They are typically affordable and provide a more personalized experience. Guesthouses can be found in popular tourist areas and are a good option for budget travelers.

3. Hostels: Hostels are ideal for budget-conscious travelers, solo travelers, and

backpackers. They offer dormitory-style accommodations with shared facilities such as bathrooms and common areas. Many hostels also have private rooms available. They are prevalent in tourist hotspots like Bangkok, Chiang Mai, and the islands.

4. Resorts: Thailand is famous for its beach resorts, particularly in destinations like Phuket, Koh Samui, and Krabi. Resorts provide a range of facilities and services, such as pools, restaurants, spas, and beachfront access. They vary in price, style, and level of luxury, catering to different budgets.

5. Villas and Vacation Rentals: For families or larger groups, renting a villa or vacation home can be an excellent choice. These properties offer more space, privacy, and often come with amenities like private pools or beach access. Platforms like Airbnb offer a variety of options throughout Thailand.

6. Eco-lodges and Nature Retreats: Thailand's natural beauty makes it an attractive destination for eco-conscious travelers. There are eco-lodges and nature retreats situated in serene settings, such as national parks and jungle areas. These accommodations prioritize sustainability and offer a closer connection to nature.

7. Homestays: Homestays provide an opportunity to stay with a local family and experience the local culture firsthand. This option allows for a more immersive and authentic travel experience. Homestays can be found in rural areas, hill tribes, and some off-the-beaten-path locations.

8. Floating Bungalows: In regions like Khao Sok National Park and parts of southern Thailand, you can find floating bungalows. These unique accommodations are situated on rivers, lakes, or coastal areas. They offer a tranquil and memorable experience, surrounded by stunning natural landscapes.

When choosing accommodation, consider factors such as location, amenities, reviews, and your budget. It's advisable to book in advance, especially during peak travel seasons, to secure your preferred choice.

# Depending on interest and budget recommended places to stay in Thailand

Thailand offers a wide range of accommodation options to suit different interests and budgets. Here are some recommended places to stay in Thailand based on popular destinations and diverse preferences:

1. Bangkok:
   - Budget: Khao San Road area or Silom district offer affordable guesthouses and budget hotels.
   - Mid-range: Sukhumvit district has a variety of hotels and serviced apartments.

- Luxury: Riverside area (Chao Phraya River) or the central business district (CBD) boast luxurious hotels and resorts.

2. Chiang Mai:
- Budget: Old Town area offers affordable guesthouses and budget hotels.
- Mid-range: Nimmanhaemin Road is a trendy neighborhood with boutique hotels and guesthouses.
- Luxury: Riverside area or the outskirts of Chiang Mai have luxurious resorts and spa retreats.

3. Phuket:
- Budget: Patong Beach or Kata Beach areas have budget-friendly guesthouses and small hotels.
- Mid-range: Karon Beach or Kamala Beach offer mid-range resorts and hotels.
- Luxury: Surin Beach or Laguna area boast high-end resorts and luxury villas.

4. Krabi:

- Budget: Ao Nang Beach area offers budget-friendly guesthouses and small hotels.

- Mid-range: Railay Beach or Klong Muang Beach have mid-range resorts and bungalows.

- Luxury: Tubkaak Beach or Phi Phi Island offer luxury resorts and private villas.

5. Koh Samui:

- Budget: Chaweng Beach or Lamai Beach areas have budget-friendly guesthouses and small hotels.

- Mid-range: Bophut Beach (Fisherman's Village) or Choeng Mon Beach offer mid-range resorts and boutique hotels.

- Luxury: Maenam Beach or Taling Ngam Beach boast luxury resorts and private villas.

6. Pattaya:

- Budget: Central Pattaya or Jomtien Beach areas have budget-friendly guesthouses and small hotels.

- Mid-range: Naklua or Pratumnak Hill offer mid-range hotels and resorts.

- Luxury: Wong Amat Beach or Koh Larn (Coral Island) have luxury resorts and private beachfront villas.

**Remember to research and book accommodation in advance, especially during peak travel seasons. Prices can vary based on the time of year, so it's recommended to compare rates and read reviews before making a decision.**

# Some of the Luxurious and affordable hotels in Thailand and how to book (Bangkok,Chiang Mai, Phuket,Koh Samui,Krabi,and Pattaya)

**Top 5 Luxurious Hotels in Bangkok:**

1. The Siam Hotel: This luxury hotel is located along the Chao Phraya River and offers a blend of traditional Thai architecture with modern comforts. Prices start at approximately $500 per night. Website: https://www.thesiamhotel.com/

2. Mandarin Oriental Bangkok: Situated on the banks of the Chao Phraya River, this iconic hotel is known for its impeccable service and

luxurious amenities. Prices start at approximately $400 per night. Website: https://www.mandarinoriental.com/bangkok

3. The Peninsula Bangkok: A riverside hotel known for its stunning views and world-class facilities. Prices start at approximately $350 per night.                    Website: https://www.peninsula.com/bangkok

4. The St. Regis Bangkok: This upscale hotel offers elegant accommodations and personalized service. Prices start at approximately $250 per night.                    Website: https://www.marriott.com/hotels/travel/bkkxr-the -st-regis-bangkok/

5. Shangri-La Hotel Bangkok: Located on the banks of the Chao Phraya River, this luxurious hotel offers spacious rooms, multiple dining options, and extensive facilities. Prices start at approximately $200 per night. Website: https://www.shangri-la.com/bangkok/shangrila/

**Top 5 Affordable Hotels in Bangkok**:

1. Ibis Bangkok Riverside: A budget-friendly hotel located on the banks of the Chao Phraya River, offering comfortable rooms and convenient amenities. Prices start at approximately $50 per night. Website: https://all.accor.com/hotel/5959/index.en.shtml

2. Holiday Inn Express Bangkok Siam: Situated in the heart of Bangkok's shopping district, this hotel offers modern rooms and easy access to attractions. Prices start at approximately $60 per night. Website: https://www.ihg.com/holidayinnexpress/hotels/us/en/bangkok/bkksm/hoteldetail

3. Novotel Bangkok Sukhumvit 20: A contemporary hotel located in the Sukhumvit area, known for its stylish rooms and rooftop pool. Prices start at approximately $70 per night. Website: https://all.accor.com/hotel/9255/index.en.shtml

4. Citin Pratunam Bangkok Hotel: This budget hotel is situated near the popular Pratunam Market and offers affordable accommodations. Prices start at approximately $40 per night. Website: https://www.citinpratunam.com/

5. Hotel Icon Bangkok: Located in the Sukhumvit area, this hotel provides comfortable rooms at reasonable prices. Prices start at approximately $50 per night. Website: https://www.hoteliconbangkok.com/

To book these hotels, you can visit their respective websites directly or use popular hotel booking platforms such as Booking.com (https://www.booking.com/) or Agoda (https://www.agoda.com/). These platforms offer a wide range of accommodation options and allow you to compare prices and read reviews before making a reservation.

**Top 5 Luxurious Hotels in Chiang Mai:**

1. Four Seasons Resort Chiang Mai: Nestled in the lush Mae Rim Valley, this luxurious resort offers stunning views, spacious villas, and impeccable service. Prices start at approximately $500 per night. Website: https://www.fourseasons.com/chiangmai/

2. Anantara Chiang Mai Resort: Located along the Mae Ping River, this elegant resort features luxurious accommodations, a serene spa, and exquisite dining options. Prices start at approximately $300 per night. Website: https://www.anantara.com/en/chiang-mai

3. Dhara Dhevi Chiang Mai: Inspired by ancient Lanna Kingdom architecture, this expansive resort showcases opulent villas, beautiful gardens, and a range of amenities. Prices start at approximately $400 per night. Website: https://www.dharadhevi.com/

4. 137 Pillars House: Housed in a restored colonial building, this boutique hotel offers luxurious suites, a tranquil spa, and a charming

atmosphere. Prices start at approximately $300 per night. Website: https://www.137pillarshotels.com/137pillarshouse/

5. Raya Heritage: Situated along the Ping River, this boutique hotel showcases contemporary Lanna design, spacious rooms, and a focus on local craftsmanship. Prices start at approximately $250 per night. Website: https://rayaheritage.com/

**Top 5 Affordable Hotels in Chiang Mai:**

1. De Chai the Deco Hotel: Located in the Nimmanhaemin area, this stylish hotel offers comfortable rooms and convenient access to shopping and dining. Prices start at approximately $60 per night. Website: https://dechaihotels.com/the-deco/

2. BED Phrasingh Hotel: Situated in the heart of the Old Town, this budget-friendly hotel features modern rooms, a rooftop pool, and a central

location. Prices start at approximately $40 per night. Website: https://www.bedphrasingh.com/

3. Rendezvous Classic House: A charming guesthouse in the Old Town area, offering cozy rooms and a traditional Thai atmosphere. Prices start at approximately $30 per night. Website: https://rendezvouschiangmai.com/

4. Green Tiger House: Located near the Tha Pae Gate, this affordable guesthouse provides comfortable accommodations and a friendly atmosphere. Prices start at approximately $25 per night. Website: https://www.greentigerhouse.com/

5. Banilah: A budget-friendly hostel situated in the Nimmanhaemin area, offering dormitory-style rooms and a social atmosphere. Prices start at approximately $15 per night. Website: https://www.banilah.com/

To book these hotels in Chiang Mai, you can visit their respective websites directly or use popular hotel booking platforms such as Booking.com (https://www.booking.com/) or Agoda (https://www.agoda.com/). These platforms offer a wide range of accommodation options and allow you to compare prices and read reviews before making a reservation.

**Top 5 Luxurious Hotels in Phuket**:

1. Trisara Phuket Villas & Residences: Situated on a private bay, this luxurious resort offers spacious villas with private pools, stunning ocean views, and exceptional service. Prices start at approximately $800 per night. Website: https://www.trisara.com/

2. Banyan Tree Phuket: Set in a lush tropical environment, this upscale resort features luxurious villas, a serene spa, and access to the Laguna Phuket Golf Club. Prices start at approximately $500 per night. Website: https://www.banyantree.com/en/thailand/phuket

3. Kata Rocks: Located in Kata Beach, this stylish resort offers modern villas with private infinity pools, panoramic sea views, and a range of luxury amenities. Prices start at approximately $400 per night. Website: https://www.katarocks.com/

4. Amanpuri: Situated on a secluded beach, this exclusive resort showcases elegant pavilions and villas, a serene spa, and a range of dining options. Prices start at approximately $1,200 per night. Website: https://www.aman.com/resorts/amanpuri

5. Rosewood Phuket: Nestled along the Emerald Bay, this luxurious resort features stylish villas, multiple dining options, and an indulgent spa. Prices start at approximately $600 per night. Website:
https://www.rosewoodhotels.com/en/phuket

**Top 5 Affordable Hotels in Phuket**:

1. Patong Lodge Hotel: Located in Patong Beach, this budget-friendly hotel offers comfortable rooms and a convenient location close to shopping and nightlife. Prices start at approximately $40 per night. Website: https://www.patonglodgehotel.com/

2. Ibis Phuket Patong: Situated in the heart of Patong Beach, this affordable hotel provides modern rooms and easy access to the beach and entertainment options. Prices start at approximately $50 per night. Website: https://all.accor.com/hotel/6538/index.en.shtml

3. The Bloc Hotel: Located in Patong Beach, this budget hotel offers clean and comfortable rooms at affordable prices. Prices start at approximately $30 per night. Website: https://www.theblochotel.com/

4. Karon Sea Sands Resort & Spa: Situated in Karon Beach, this mid-range hotel offers comfortable rooms, a pool, and easy access to

the beach. Prices start at approximately $60 per night. Website: https://www.karonseasand.com/

5. Phuket Graceland Resort & Spa: Located in Patong Beach, this affordable resort features comfortable rooms, multiple swimming pools, and a range of facilities. Prices start at approximately $70 per night. Website: https://www.phuketgraceland.com/

To book these hotels in Phuket, you can visit their respective websites directly or use popular hotel booking platforms such as Booking.com (https://www.booking.com/) or Agoda (https://www.agoda.com/). These platforms offer a wide range of accommodation options and allow you to compare prices and read reviews before making a reservation.

Top 5 Luxurious Hotels in Koh Samui:

1. Four Seasons Resort Koh Samui:
   - Price: Starting from $900 per night
   - Website: www.fourseasons.com/kohsamui

2. Banyan Tree Samui:
   - Price: Starting from $800 per night
   -                                 Website:
www.banyantree.com/en/thailand/samui

3. The Ritz-Carlton, Koh Samui:
   - Price: Starting from $700 per night
   - Website: www.ritzcarlton.com/kohsamui

4. Six Senses Samui:
   - Price: Starting from $600 per night
   - Website: www.sixsenses.com/resorts/samui

5. Conrad Koh Samui:
   - Price: Starting from $500 per night
   - Website: www.conradkohsamui.com

Top 5 Affordable Hotels in Koh Samui:

1. Amarin Samui Hotel:
   - Price: Starting from $60 per night
   - Website: www.amarinsamuihotel.com

2. Chaweng Noi Pool Villa:
   - Price: Starting from $70 per night
   - Website: www.chawengnoipoolvilla.com

3. Lamai Wanta Beach Resort:
   - Price: Starting from $80 per night
   - Website: www.lamaiwanta.com

4. Ibis Samui Bophut:
   - Price: Starting from $90 per night
                                    - Website:
   www.accorhotels.com/ibis-samui-bophut

5. Chaweng Garden Beach Resort:
   - Price: Starting from $100 per night
   - Website: www.chawenggarden.com

Please note that prices are approximate and may vary depending on the season and availability. It's always a good idea to visit the hotel websites or use hotel booking platforms like Booking.com or Expedia to get the most up-to-date prices and make reservations.

Top 5 Luxurious Hotels in Krabi:

1. Rayavadee Resort:
   - Price: Starting from $500 per night
   - Website: www.rayavadee.com

2. Phulay Bay, a Ritz-Carlton Reserve:
   - Price: Starting from $600 per night
   - Website: www.ritzcarlton.com/phulaybay

3. Dusit Thani Krabi Beach Resort:
   - Price: Starting from $400 per night
   - Website: www.dusit.com/dusitthani/krabibeachresort

4. Tubkaak Krabi Boutique Resort:
   - Price: Starting from $300 per night
   - Website: www.tubkaakresort.com

5. Sofitel Krabi Phokeethra Golf & Spa Resort:
   - Price: Starting from $250 per night
   - Website: www.sofitelkrabiphokeethra.com

Top 5 Affordable Hotels in Krabi:

1. Aonang Phu Petra Resort:
   - Price: Starting from $70 per night
   - Website: www.aonangphupetra.com

2. Anyavee Tubkaek Beach Resort:
   - Price: Starting from $80 per night
   -                               Website:
www.anyaveetubkaekbeachresort.com

3. Red Ginger Chic Resort:
   - Price: Starting from $90 per night
   - Website: www.redgingerkrabi.com

4. Sand Sea Resort:
   - Price: Starting from $100 per night
   - Website: www.sandsearesortkrabi.com

5. Ibis Styles Krabi Ao Nang:
   - Price: Starting from $110 per night
   -                               Website:
www.accorhotels.com/ibis-styles-krabi-ao-nang

As with any hotel reservations, prices can vary depending on the season and availability. It is recommended to visit the hotel websites or use hotel booking platforms like Booking.com or Expedia to get the most accurate and up-to-date prices for your desired dates.

Top 5 Luxurious Hotels in Pattaya:

1. Royal Wing Suites & Spa:
   - Price: Starting from $300 per night
   - Website: www.royalcliff.com/royal-wing

2. InterContinental Pattaya Resort:
   - Price: Starting from $250 per night
   -                           Website: www.ihg.com/intercontinental/pattaya

3. Hilton Pattaya:
   - Price: Starting from $200 per night
   - Website: www.hilton.com/pattaya

4. AVANI Pattaya Resort:
   - Price: Starting from $150 per night

- Website: www.avanihotels.com/pattaya

5. Cape Dara Resort:
   - Price: Starting from $120 per night
   - Website: www.capedarapattaya.com

Top 5 Affordable Hotels in Pattaya:

1. Holiday Inn Express Pattaya Central:
   - Price: Starting from $50 per night
                              -        Website:
www.ihg.com/holidayinnexpress/pattayacentral

2. Ibis Pattaya:
   - Price: Starting from $40 per night
   - Website: www.accorhotels.com/ibis-pattaya

3. Aya Boutique Hotel Pattaya:
   - Price: Starting from $30 per night
   - Website: www.ayaresidence.com

4. LK The Empress Pattaya:
   - Price: Starting from $25 per night
   - Website: www.lkpattaya.com

5. April Suites Pattaya:
   - Price: Starting from $20 per night
   - Website: www.aprilsuites.com

Please note that prices are approximate and may vary depending on the season and availability. It's always a good idea to visit the hotel websites or use hotel booking platforms like Booking.com or Expedia to get the most up-to-date prices and make reservations

**More of the best hotels in Thailand in 2023:**

1. Banyan Tree Bangkok - A luxurious hotel in Sathorn with stunning city views and world-class amenities.

2. Anantara Chiang Mai Resort - A serene oasis in the heart of Chiang Mai that combines contemporary style with traditional Thai design.

3. Keemala Resort Phuket - A unique and luxurious resort in Kamala that offers guests an unforgettable jungle experience.

4. The Siam Hotel Bangkok - A five-star hotel in Bangkok that showcases elegant and classic Thai design in a serene and peaceful atmosphere.

5. Amanpuri Phuket - A lavish resort in Phuket that boasts stunning beach scenery and top-notch services.

6. Rayavadee Krabi - A secluded beachfront resort located in Railay, Krabi that offers guests tranquility and natural beauty.

7. Phulay Bay Ritz-Carlton Reserve Krabi - A luxurious retreat in the beautifulsouthern coast of Thailand, Phulay Bay Ritz-Carlton Reserve Krabi offers stunning views of the Andaman Sea and breathtaking surroundings.

# Food choices

Street Food: Thailand is famous for its vibrant street food culture. You can find a wide variety of delicious and affordable dishes at street food stalls throughout the country.
Some popular street food items include pad Thai, som tam (papaya salad), grilled satay, and mango sticky rice.

Fine Dining: Bangkok, the capital city, is known for its high-end dining scene. You'll find numerous fine dining restaurants offering both Thai and international cuisines. Gaggan, Le Du, Nahm, and Bo.lan are some of the well-known fine dining establishments in Bangkok.

Seafood: Since Thailand has a long coastline, seafood is abundant and popular. Coastal areas like Phuket, Krabi, and Pattaya are known for their fresh seafood restaurants. These restaurants often offer a wide range of seafood dishes, including grilled fish, prawns, crab, and shellfish.

Northern Thai Cuisine: Chiang Mai, in the north of Thailand, is famous for its distinctive cuisine. You can try dishes like khao soi (curry noodle soup), sai ua (northern Thai sausage), and gaeng hang lay (pork curry) at local restaurants and street stalls in Chiang Mai.

Vegetarian and Vegan: Thailand is also known for its vegetarian and vegan-friendly options. Many restaurants and street food stalls offer plant-based dishes and cater to dietary preferences. Some well-known vegetarian and vegan restaurants in Bangkok include May Veggie Home, Broccoli Revolution, and Veganerie.

# List of some eateries and restaurants in Thailand

1. Gaggan (Bangkok) - Known for its innovative and progressive Indian cuisine, Gaggan has consistently ranked among the top restaurants in Asia. It offers a unique dining experience with a tasting menu that showcases Chef Gaggan Anand's culinary creativity.

2. Nahm (Bangkok) - Renowned for its traditional Thai cuisine with a modern twist, Nahm has received critical acclaim. The restaurant focuses on showcasing the rich flavors and ingredients of Thai food in a contemporary setting.

3. Bo.lan (Bangkok) - Committed to sustainable practices and using organic ingredients, Bo.lan offers a fine dining experience featuring refined

Thai dishes. Their menu highlights regional flavors and seasonal produce.

4. Le Du (Bangkok) - Known for its innovative approach to Thai cuisine, Le Du combines traditional Thai ingredients with modern cooking techniques. The restaurant offers a tasting menu that showcases Chef Ton's culinary expertise.

5. Blue Elephant (Bangkok) - Located in a beautiful colonial-style building, Blue Elephant is renowned for its authentic Thai cuisine and elegant ambiance. They offer cooking classes as well as a la carte dining options.

6. Sorn (Bangkok) - Specializing in Southern Thai cuisine, Sorn is celebrated for its flavorsome dishes and attention to detail. The restaurant focuses on preserving traditional recipes and using locally sourced ingredients.

7. Issaya Siamese Club (Bangkok) - Set in a charming Thai villa, Issaya Siamese Club offers a unique dining experience with a menu inspired

by Thai flavors and international influences. This restaurant is known for its creative dishes and beautiful presentation.

8. David's Kitchen (Chiang Mai) - Led by Chef David Gordon, David's Kitchen is a highly regarded restaurant in Chiang Mai. It offers a blend of European and Thai cuisines, featuring dishes made with fresh local ingredients.

9. Huen Phen (Chiang Mai) - Located in the old city of Chiang Mai, Huen Phen is a popular restaurant serving traditional Northern Thai cuisine. It offers a range of flavorful dishes that highlight the region's unique flavors.

10. Supanniga Eating Room (Bangkok and Khon Kaen) - With multiple locations, Supanniga Eating Room is known for its authentic Thai dishes, focusing on recipes passed down through generations. They offer a cozy and casual dining atmosphere.

**Websites to book reservations**
1.https://www.opentable.co.th/c/thailand-restaurants.
2.https://www.foodpanda.co.th/
3.https://www.chope.co/bangkok-restaurants?lang=en_US
4.https://www.similarweb.com/website/wongnai.com/#overview

# Vegetarians and vegans choices

Thailand offers a variety of delicious vegetarian and vegan options, and it's generally easy to find meals that cater to these dietary preferences. Here are some choices for vegetarians and vegans in Thailand:

1. Thai Cuisine: Thai cuisine is known for its vibrant flavors and extensive use of herbs, spices, and vegetables. Many traditional Thai dishes can be easily modified to be vegetarian or vegan by substituting meat or seafood with tofu, vegetables, or mock meats. Some popular

vegetarian-friendly Thai dishes include Pad Thai (stir-fried noodles), Green Curry, Tom Yum Soup (request without shrimp), and Som Tam (papaya salad).

2. Fresh Fruit: Thailand is abundant in tropical fruits, and they make for delicious and healthy snacks. Enjoy a variety of fruits such as mangoes, pineapples, watermelons, dragon fruits, and bananas. You can find fresh fruit sold by street vendors, at markets, or in fruit smoothie stands.

3. Vegetarian and Vegan Restaurants: Thailand has a growing number of dedicated vegetarian and vegan restaurants, especially in major cities like Bangkok, Chiang Mai, and Phuket. These establishments offer a wide range of plant-based dishes, from traditional Thai cuisine to international and fusion options. Some well-known vegetarian and vegan restaurants in Thailand include May Kaidee, Veganerie, and Ethos.

4. Street Food: Thailand's street food scene is a paradise for vegetarians and vegans. You can find various vegetarian-friendly options such as vegetable spring rolls, deep-fried tofu, grilled corn on the cob, fresh fruit shakes, and coconut-based desserts. Just communicate your dietary preferences to the vendors and ask them to omit any non-vegetarian ingredients like fish sauce or meat.

5. Buddhist Temples: Many Buddhist temples in Thailand offer vegetarian or vegan food as part of their daily offerings or in their on-site restaurants. These meals are often served buffet-style and are suitable for vegetarians and vegans. Some well-known temples with vegetarian food options include Wat Arun and Wat Pho in Bangkok and Wat Suan Dok in Chiang Mai.

6. Western and International Cuisine: Thailand's popular tourist destinations often have a wide range of international restaurants that cater to different dietary preferences. You can find

vegetarian and vegan-friendly options such as Italian, Mexican, Indian, Middle Eastern, and Mediterranean cuisines. These restaurants usually have vegetarian or vegan menu items clearly labeled.

7. Food Markets and Supermarkets: Food markets and supermarkets in Thailand offer a variety of fresh produce, tofu, plant-based ingredients, and packaged vegetarian and vegan products. You can buy ingredients to cook your meals if you have access to a kitchen or grab pre-packaged vegetarian snacks or meals.

When dining out, it's helpful to learn a few key phrases in Thai to communicate your dietary preferences clearly. For vegetarians, you can say "mang-sa-wi-rat" (มังสวิรัติ) which means "vegetarian," and for vegans, you can say "gin jay" (กินเจ) which means "eat vegan."

Thailand's culinary landscape offers a wide array of options for vegetarians and vegans, ensuring you can enjoy the flavors of the country while adhering to your dietary preferences.

# Car rental services in Thailand

Here are some car rental companies in Thailand:

1. Budget Rent a Car Thailand
2. Avis Car Rental Thailand
3. Hertz Thailand
4. Thrifty Car Rental Thailand
5. Sixt Rent a Car Thailand
6. Europcar Thailand
7. National Car Rental Thailand
8. Thai Rent A Car
9. Bizcar Rental
10. Yesaway Car Rental Thailand

Please note that availability of these companies and their services may vary depending on the location in Thailand.

# Emergency services in Thailand

In Thailand, the emergency number is 191 for police, 1669 for medical emergencies, and 199 for firefighters.

If you are a tourist, you can also contact the Tourist Police at 1155 for any non-emergency support or assistance, such as lost passports, lost property, or general information.

Thailand also has many hospital facilities that cater to tourists. Some of the highly recommended hospitals for tourists include Bumrungrad International Hospital in Bangkok
Bangkok Hospital Phuket
Chiang Mai Ram Hospital in Chiang Mai.
These hospitals are equipped with modern facilities and have English-speaking staff to assist you.

In case of any emergency, do not hesitate to contact the relevant authorities for prompt assistance. It's always recommended to keep the emergency numbers and contact information of your country's embassy or consulate in Thailand with you, in case you need their assistance during an emergency situation.

# Group tours

When it comes to group tours in Thailand, there are several reputable agencies that offer well-organized and reliable services. However, it's important to note that the availability and specific offerings of tour agencies may change over time. Therefore, it's advisable to research and verify the current status and reliability of any agency before making a booking. Here are a few trusted tour agencies in Thailand that have consistently received positive reviews:

1. Intrepid Travel: Intrepid Travel is a globally recognized tour operator known for its

sustainable and responsible travel practices. They offer a variety of group tours in Thailand, ranging from cultural exploration to adventure trips. Their itineraries often focus on local experiences, small-group sizes, and supporting local communities.

2. G Adventures: G Adventures is another well-regarded tour company with a wide range of group tours in Thailand. They emphasize authentic experiences, small-group travel, and sustainability. Their itineraries cater to different travel styles and budgets, from budget-friendly options to more premium adventures.

3. Urban Adventures: Urban Adventures specializes in immersive day tours and local experiences. They offer a variety of day trips and city tours in major Thai cities like Bangkok, Chiang Mai, and Phuket. These tours focus on exploring local neighborhoods, trying street food, and engaging with the local culture.

4. Smiling Albino: Smiling Albino is a boutique tour operator that provides tailor-made, private, and small-group tours in Thailand. They offer personalized itineraries, cultural experiences, and off-the-beaten-path adventures. Smiling Albino is known for its attention to detail and customer service.

5. EXO Travel: EXO Travel is a leading tour operator with a strong presence in Southeast Asia, including Thailand. They offer a range of group tours, private tours, and custom itineraries. EXO Travel focuses on providing authentic experiences, knowledgeable guides, and high-quality service.

6. Contiki

7. TruTravels

8.INTRO Travel

Remember to carefully review the itineraries, inclusions, and terms and conditions of any tour agency before making a booking. Consider factors such as group size, activities offered, accommodation standards, transportation arrangements, and the reputation of the agency.

It's also helpful to read reviews from previous travelers to gauge their experiences and satisfaction with the tour agency.

Additionally, when booking a group tour, be sure to check the latest travel advisories and health guidelines related to COVID-19. It's essential to prioritize your safety and comply with any necessary travel restrictions or protocols in place.

# Telecommunication

Telecommunication for tourists in Thailand is well-developed, and there are several options available to stay connected during your visit. Here's an overview of telecommunication services for tourists in Thailand:

1. SIM Cards: Purchasing a local SIM card is a popular and cost-effective option. You can buy SIM cards at the airport, convenience stores, or mobile service provider shops throughout

Thailand. The major telecom companies in Thailand are AIS, TrueMove H, and dtac. These SIM cards typically come with prepaid packages offering data, voice calls, and SMS. Prices for SIM cards vary depending on the chosen package and provider.

2. Tourist SIM Cards: Some telecom providers offer specific tourist SIM cards tailored to the needs of travelers. These SIM cards often include a set amount of data, free calls, and other benefits. They are available at airports, shopping malls, and mobile service provider shops.

3. Internet Access: Thailand has widespread 4G and 5G coverage in major cities and popular tourist destinations. You can access the internet via mobile data on your smartphone or by connecting to Wi-Fi networks available at hotels, cafes, and public areas. Many hotels and accommodations provide free Wi-Fi access to their guests.

4. Wi-Fi Hotspots: Thailand offers numerous Wi-Fi hotspots in public areas, shopping malls, restaurants, and cafes. Some locations offer free Wi-Fi, while others may require a password or registration. Look for signs or ask the staff for Wi-Fi availability and access details.

5. Mobile Apps: Various mobile apps can assist you in staying connected and navigating Thailand. For example, messaging apps like LINE and WhatsApp are widely used for communication. Additionally, transportation apps like Grab and food delivery apps like GrabFood or Foodpanda can be convenient during your stay.

6.AT&T:Yes, AT&T does provide international roaming services in Thailand. However, it's best to check with AT&T directly to confirm the specifics of their coverage and any associated fees or restrictions. You can contact AT&T customer support or visit their website for more information.

Before purchasing a SIM card or mobile package, compare the available options from different providers to find the one that best suits your needs in terms of data, voice calls, and duration of stay. Ensure your smartphone is unlocked and compatible with Thai networks. Also, remember to carry your passport as it may be required for SIM card registration.

## Activities for family.

Thailand offers a wide range of activities that are perfect for families. Here are some popular options:

1. Explore Bangkok: Visit the Grand Palace, Wat Arun, and Wat Phra Kaew. Take a boat ride along the Chao Phraya River and explore the vibrant markets and street food scene.

2. Enjoy the Beaches: Head to popular beach destinations like Phuket, Krabi, or Koh Samui. Relax on the beautiful beaches, go swimming or

snorkeling, and indulge in water sports like kayaking or jet skiing.

3. Visit Chiang Mai: Explore the cultural heritage of Chiang Mai by visiting temples like Wat Phra That Doi Suthep and Wat Chedi Luang. Engage in activities like elephant sanctuaries, ziplining, or taking a cooking class.

4. Wildlife Encounters: Take your family to Khao Yai National Park or Samutprakarn Crocodile Farm and Zoo to experience Thailand's diverse wildlife. Go on guided tours or safaris to spot elephants, tigers, monkeys, and various bird species.

5. Water Parks: Have a fun-filled day at one of Thailand's water parks, such as Cartoon Network Amazone in Pattaya or Vana Nava Water Jungle in Hua Hin. Enjoy thrilling water slides, wave pools, and lazy rivers.

6. Floating Markets: Visit the famous floating markets like Damnoen Saduak or Amphawa near

Bangkok. Take a boat tour, shop for local products, and enjoy delicious Thai street food.

7. Thai Cultural Shows: Attend traditional Thai cultural shows like Siam Niramit in Bangkok or the Khon Dance Performance in Chiang Mai. These performances showcase traditional dances, music, and martial arts.

8. Waterfalls and Nature Trails: Explore the natural beauty of Thailand by visiting waterfalls such as Erawan Falls or Namtok Phlio National Park. Enjoy hiking, swimming, and picnicking amidst lush green surroundings.

9. Theme Parks: Visit amusement parks like Dream World or Safari World in Bangkok. Enjoy thrilling rides, animal shows, and live entertainment suitable for all ages.

10. Thai Cooking Classes: Enroll in a family-friendly cooking class where you can learn to prepare authentic Thai dishes. Bond

with your loved ones as you discover the secrets of Thai cuisine.

Remember to check the availability and accessibility of these activities before planning your trip, as some options may vary or have specific requirements.

# Do's and don'ts

When visiting Thailand, it's important to be aware of the local customs and etiquette. Here are some do's and don'ts to keep in mind:

Do's:
1. Do dress modestly when visiting temples or religious sites. It is respectful to cover your shoulders and knees.
2. Do greet people with the traditional Thai greeting called "wai." Place your palms together in a prayer-like gesture and slightly bow your head.

3. Do remove your shoes before entering someone's home, temples, or certain businesses, as it is a customary practice.

4. Do try to learn a few basic Thai phrases, such as "hello" (sawasdee kha for females, sawasdee krab for males) and "thank you" (khob khun kha for females, khob khun krab for males). It shows respect and can go a long way in communicating with locals.

5. Do be respectful when interacting with Thai royalty, symbols, and institutions. Criticizing or disrespecting the royal family is illegal and can lead to severe consequences.

6. Do be mindful of your actions and avoid public displays of affection, especially in more conservative areas.

7. Do haggle when shopping at markets or street vendors, but do so in a friendly and polite manner. It's part of the culture, and you may get a better deal.

8. Do try the local cuisine and street food. Thailand is known for its delicious dishes, and exploring the local food scene can be a fantastic experience.

Don'ts:

1. Don't disrespect Buddha images or sacred objects. Treat them with reverence and avoid inappropriate behavior like climbing on statues or using them as props for photos.

2. Don't touch people on the head, as it is considered disrespectful in Thai culture. The head is considered sacred.

3. Don't point your feet directly at people or use them to gesture or touch objects. The feet are considered the lowest part of the body and are seen as unclean.

4. Don't show anger or lose your temper in public. Thais value harmony and "saving face," so maintaining composure and resolving conflicts calmly is important.

5. Don't engage in illegal activities, such as drug use or trafficking. Thailand has strict laws and severe penalties for such offenses.

6. Don't litter or disrespect the environment. Keep the surroundings tidy and dispose all waste properly.

7. Don't talk about the royal family or engage in political discussions unless you have a deep understanding of the situation and the potential consequences.
8. Don't ignore the local customs and norms. Observe and adapt to the local way of life to show respect and avoid unintentional offense.

Remember, these are general guidelines, and customs may vary depending on the specific region or situation within Thailand. Being respectful, open-minded, and willing to learn will help you have a positive and enjoyable experience in the country.

# 7 day itenary

Here's a sample 7-day itinerary for Thailand, focusing on popular destinations such as Bangkok and the nearby islands:

Day 1: Bangkok
- Arrive in Bangkok and settle into your accommodation.

- Explore the Grand Palace and Wat Phra Kaew (Temple of the Emerald Buddha).
- Explore Wat Pho (Temple of the Reclining Buddha) and its famous giant reclining Buddha statue.
- Take a boat ride along the Chao Phraya River and explore the vibrant Chinatown.
- Enjoy the nightlife and street food scene in the lively Sukhumvit area.

Day 2: Ayutthaya Day Trip
- Take a day trip to Ayutthaya, an ancient capital city located north of Bangkok.
- Explore the UNESCO World Heritage Site, Ayutthaya Historical Park, and visit the ancient temples and ruins.
- Take a boat ride along the Chao Phraya River and enjoy the scenic views.
- Return to Bangkok in the evening and relax or explore the city's nightlife.

Day 3: Phuket
- Fly from Bangkok to Phuket, a popular island destination in southern Thailand.

- Relax on the beautiful beaches of Patong, Karon, or Kata.
- Explore the Old Town area of Phuket with its charming Sino-Portuguese architecture.
- Enjoy the vibrant nightlife in Patong, known for its bustling streets and entertainment options.

Day 4: Phi Phi Islands
- Take a day trip to the stunning Phi Phi Islands from Phuket.
- Enjoy snorkeling or diving in the crystal-clear waters around Phi Phi Don and Phi Phi Leh islands.
- Visit Maya Bay, made popular by the movie titled "The Beach."
- Relax on the beaches, swim, and soak up the sun.
- Return to Phuket in the evening.

Day 5: Chiang Mai
- Fly from Phuket to Chiang Mai, a cultural hub in northern Thailand.

- Visit the sacred Wat Phra That Doi Suthep, located on a hill with panoramic views of the city.
- Explore the Old City of Chiang Mai and its temples, including Wat Chedi Luang and Wat Phra Singh.
- Experience the famous Night Bazaar, where you can shop for local handicrafts, souvenirs, and sample delicious street food.

Day 6: Elephant Sanctuary and Thai Cooking Class
- Spend the morning at an ethical elephant sanctuary, where you can learn about and interact with elephants in a responsible way.
- Enjoy feeding, bathing, and observing these magnificent creatures.
- In the afternoon, join a Thai cooking class and learn how to prepare traditional Thai dishes.
- Enjoy the fruits of your labor by indulging in the delicious food you cooked.

Day 7: Bangkok Departure
- Fly from Chiang Mai back to Bangkok.

- Visit the floating market at Damnoen Saduak, where you can experience the vibrant atmosphere and purchase local goods.
- Explore the shopping malls of Bangkok, such as Siam Paragon or MBK Center, for some last-minute shopping.
- Enjoy a farewell dinner at a rooftop restaurant with panoramic views of the city.
- Depart from Bangkok or continue your journey in Thailand.

Remember to check the current travel restrictions, flight schedules, and availability of attractions before planning your trip. This itinerary can be customized based on your preferences and the time of year you plan to visit Thailand.

# Travel insurance

Travel insurance is a type of insurance coverage that helps protect you financially against unexpected events and expenses that may occur while you are traveling. It provides coverage for a range of potential risks and can offer peace of mind during your trip. Here are some key points to know about travel insurance:

1. Coverage: Travel insurance typically offers coverage for various aspects, including:

- Trip cancellation or interruption: Reimbursement for non-refundable trip expenses if you need to cancel or cut short your trip due to covered reasons, such as illness, injury, or other unforeseen events.

- Medical expenses: Coverage for medical emergencies, illness, or injuries that occur during your trip. This can include hospitalization, doctor visits, medications, and emergency medical evacuation.

- Baggage and personal belongings: Protection for lost, stolen, or damaged baggage and personal items.

- Travel delays: Reimbursement for additional expenses incurred due to travel delays, such as accommodation, meals, or transportation.

- Travel assistance: Access to 24/7 emergency assistance services for travel-related problems or emergencies.

2. Types of Travel Insurance:
- Single-Trip Insurance: Covers a specific trip for a designated period.
- Annual/Multi-Trip Insurance: Provides coverage for multiple trips within a year.
- International and Domestic Insurance: Options available for both international and domestic travel.

3. Considerations when purchasing travel insurance:
- Trip details: Provide accurate trip information, including travel dates, destinations, and the total trip cost, to ensure appropriate coverage.
- Coverage limits: Review the policy to understand the coverage limits and exclusions for various aspects, such as medical expenses or baggage coverage.

- Pre-existing conditions: Check if pre-existing medical conditions are covered or if you need to purchase additional coverage.

- Activities and sports: If you plan to engage in adventure activities or sports, ensure that they are covered under the policy.

- Compare policies: Shop around, compare different policies, and understand the terms and conditions before making a decision.

4. Costs: The cost of travel insurance varies based on factors such as the duration of the trip, the coverage selected, the age of the traveler, and the destination. It's essential to balance the coverage provided with your budget.

5. Policy Exclusions: Travel insurance policies have exclusions, meaning there are situations or circumstances that are not covered. Pre-existing medical issues, risky activities, and travel to nations where travel restrictions are in effect are typical exclusions..

6. Claims Process: Familiarize yourself with the claims process and keep all necessary documentation, such as receipts, medical reports, and police reports, to support your claim if needed.

Remember to carefully read the policy documents, including terms, conditions, and exclusions, to understand the coverage provided by a specific travel insurance plan. It's also advisable to consult with a licensed insurance professional to assess your specific needs and determine the most suitable travel insurance for your trip.

## Saving money in Thailand

Thailand can be a budget-friendly destination if you plan wisely and make smart choices. Here are some tips to help you save money while traveling in Thailand:

1. Travel during the shoulder or off-peak seasons: Prices for flights, accommodations, and

attractions tend to be lower during the shoulder or off-peak seasons. Consider visiting Thailand during less crowded periods, such as the months of May to September.

2. Look for affordable accommodations: Thailand offers a wide range of accommodations to suit various budgets. Consider staying in guesthouses, hostels, or budget hotels, especially in less touristy areas, to save on accommodation costs. Booking in advance or using hotel comparison websites can help you find the best deals.

3. Eat like a local: Street food is not only delicious but also affordable in Thailand. Explore the local markets and street food stalls to experience authentic Thai cuisine at lower prices compared to restaurants. Look for places busy with locals, as it often indicates good quality and reasonable prices. Additionally, consider dining at local restaurants away from tourist hotspots to save money.

4. Use public transportation: Public transportation options like buses, trains, and the Bangkok Skytrain (BTS) or Bangkok Metro (MRT) are cost-effective ways to get around Thailand. They are generally cheaper than taxis or private transportation services. Tuk-tuks and songthaews (shared taxis) can also be inexpensive alternatives for short distances.

5. Bargain at markets and negotiate prices: Haggling is a common practice in Thailand, particularly at markets and with street vendors. Don't be afraid to negotiate prices, especially when buying souvenirs, clothing, or other items at local markets. Remember to be friendly and respectful while haggling.

6. Limit alcohol consumption and nightlife expenses: Alcoholic beverages, especially imported ones, can be relatively expensive in Thailand. Consider limiting your alcohol consumption or opting for local beers or cocktails. Additionally, be mindful of the costs

associated with nightlife activities, such as club cover charges and drinks in touristy areas.

7. Join group tours or activities: Booking group tours or activities can be more cost-effective than arranging private tours. Many tour operators offer group packages that include transportation, entrance fees, and a guide, which can help save money compared to organizing everything individually.

8. Explore free or low-cost attractions: Thailand has numerous free or low-cost attractions that provide rich cultural experiences. Explore temples, public parks, and local markets, or enjoy the natural beauty of Thailand's beaches and national parks without spending a significant amount.

9. Stay hydrated with tap water or refillable bottles: In many parts of Thailand, tap water is not safe to drink. However, you can save money on bottled water by using refillable water bottles and purchasing bottled water from convenience

stores instead of restaurants or tourist areas, where prices may be higher.

10. Research and plan ahead: Researching your destination and planning your activities in advance can help you identify affordable options and avoid unnecessary expenses. Look for discounts, promotions, and deals on accommodations, attractions, and transportation.

Remember, while it's important to save money, also prioritize your safety, comfort, and overall enjoyment of your trip. Finding a balance between saving money and experiencing the best of Thailand will ensure a memorable and budget-friendly adventure.

# Bangkok

the vibrant capital of Thailand, serves as the gateway to the country's rich culture and traditions. Here are some highlights of exploring Bangkok:

1. Exploring the Grand Palace and Wat Phra Kaew:
The Grand Palace is a majestic complex that served as the residence of Thai kings for generations. Within the palace grounds, you'll find the famous Wat Phra Kaew (Temple of the Emerald Buddha), which houses a revered Buddha image carved from a single piece of jade. Marvel at the intricate architecture, exquisite details, and vibrant colors of this sacred site.The Grand Palace and Wat Phra Kaew are two of the most iconic and important landmarks in Bangkok, Thailand. Let me take you on a virtual tour of these magnificent places!

The Grand Palace is a vast complex that served as the official residence of the Kings of Siam (and later Thailand) for over 150 years. Built in 1782, it is a stunning example of Thai architecture and craftsmanship. The palace complex covers an area of 218,400 square meters and is divided into several sections.

As you enter the palace, you'll first come across the Outer Court, which was used for administrative purposes. Here, you'll find various government offices and ceremonial buildings. One of the notable buildings in this area is the Chakri Maha Prasat Hall, which combines traditional Thai elements with European architectural styles.

Moving further into the palace, you'll reach the Middle Court, where the most important residential and state buildings are located. The most prominent structure here is the Phra Maha Monthien Buildings, which were used for various royal functions and ceremonies. You can also explore the Borom Phiman Mansion, which served as the residence of the King Rama VIII.

Finally, you'll reach the Inner Court, where the sacred Wat Phra Kaew (Temple of the Emerald Buddha) is located. This temple is considered the most sacred in Thailand and houses the highly revered Emerald Buddha, which is actually made of jade. The Emerald Buddha is a symbol of prosperity and protection for the Thai people.

As you enter the temple complex, you'll be surrounded by intricate details, colorful murals, and beautiful statues. The architecture of the temple is breathtaking, with spires, pagodas, and gilded decorations. Remember to dress modestly, as Wat Phra Kaew is a religious site, and visitors are expected to show respect.

Inside the main hall, you'll find the Emerald Buddha enshrined on a golden pedestal. The statue itself is relatively small, but it holds immense cultural and religious significance. The

Emerald Buddha's robes are changed three times a year by the King himself to correspond with the changing seasons.

Exploring the Grand Palace and Wat Phra Kaew is like stepping into a rich tapestry of Thai history, art, and spirituality. The intricate architecture, the vibrant colors, and the serene atmosphere make it a truly remarkable experience.

Remember to allocate enough time for your visit, as there is much to see within the complex. It's also advisable to arrive early to beat the crowds and make the most of your visit.

2. The Spiritual Serenity of Wat Arun:
Located on the banks of the Chao Phraya River, Wat Arun (Temple of Dawn) is one of Bangkok's most iconic landmarks. This temple is known for its stunning Khmer-style prang (tower) adorned with colorful porcelain tiles. Climb to the top for a breathtaking view of the river and the cityscape, especially during sunset.

Wat Arun, also known as the Temple of Dawn, is another magnificent temple in Bangkok that offers a unique spiritual experience. Let's embark on a virtual journey to discover the spiritual serenity of Wat Arun.

Located on the western bank of the Chao Phraya River, Wat Arun stands as an iconic landmark with its towering spires and intricate architectural details. The temple's name, "Arun," means "dawn" in Thai, and it is believed that the first light of the morning beautifully illuminates the temple, creating a captivating sight.

The central feature of Wat Arun is its central prang (spire), which reaches a height of about 79 meters (259 feet). The prang is adorned with colorful porcelain tiles, reflecting the sunlight and creating a shimmering effect. Climbing to the top of the prang allows visitors to enjoy panoramic views of the Chao Phraya River and the surrounding area.

Wat Arun is deeply rooted in Thai mythology and symbolism. The temple represents Mount Meru, the center of the universe in Hindu and Buddhist cosmology. Its design incorporates elements of both Hindu and Buddhist traditions, showcasing the rich cultural heritage of Thailand.

As you explore the temple complex, you'll come across various statues, shrines, and pavilions dedicated to different deities. One of the notable features is the Ordination Hall, which houses a Buddha image that was brought from Ayutthaya, the ancient capital of Thailand.

Wat Arun also holds great spiritual significance for the Thai people. Many locals come here to pay their respects, offer prayers, and participate in religious ceremonies. The serene ambiance of the temple, coupled with the sound of chanting and the fragrance of incense, creates an atmosphere of tranquility and devotion.

To fully appreciate the spiritual serenity of Wat Arun, it's best to visit during quieter times, preferably in the morning or late afternoon. This allows you to immerse yourself in the peacefulness of the temple and have a more intimate experience with its spiritual essence.

Whether you visit Wat Arun for its architectural splendor, its cultural significance, or its spiritual aura, it promises to leave a lasting impression. The combination of its graceful design, the riverside location, and the sense of tranquility it evokes make Wat Arun a truly remarkable destination.

3. Vibrant Markets and Street Food Delights:
Bangkok is renowned for its vibrant markets and delicious street food scene. Let's take a virtual tour and explore the exciting markets and street food delights the city has to offer!

1. Chatuchak Weekend Market: This is one of the largest and most famous markets in Bangkok, attracting both locals and tourists. It's

a treasure trove of shopping, with thousands of stalls offering a wide range of products, including clothing, accessories, handicrafts, home decor, and much more. You can also find delicious street food here, such as grilled skewers, pad Thai, mango sticky rice, and refreshing fruit smoothies.

2. Chinatown (Yaowarat): Located in the heart of Bangkok, Chinatown is a bustling neighborhood known for its vibrant street food scene. As you stroll through the narrow alleys, you'll encounter countless food stalls and restaurants serving up Chinese and Thai delicacies. Don't miss out on dishes like dim sum, crispy pork belly, fresh seafood, and exotic fruits.

3. Damnoen Saduak Floating Market: For a unique shopping experience, visit the floating market at Damnoen Saduak, located just outside Bangkok. Vendors sell their goods from small boats, creating a colorful and lively atmosphere. You can buy fresh fruits, vegetables, snacks,

souvenirs, and even have a boat ride through the picturesque canals.

4. Or Tor Kor Market: If you're a food lover, Or Tor Kor Market is a must-visit. This indoor market is known for its high-quality produce, including a wide variety of tropical fruits, vegetables, spices, and seafood. You'll also find ready-to-eat Thai dishes, snacks, and desserts that will tantalize your taste buds.

5. Sukhumvit Soi 38 Night Market: Located in the bustling Sukhumvit area, this night market is a haven for street food enthusiasts. From succulent grilled meats to spicy noodles, aromatic curries, and refreshing Thai iced tea, you'll find a wide array of dishes to satisfy your cravings.

6. Talad Rot Fai (Train Night Market): Situated near the Chatuchak area, Talad Rot Fai is a vintage-themed night market that offers a unique shopping experience. Aside from the eclectic mix of vintage clothing, antiques, and

collectibles, the market is also renowned for its delicious street food. Indulge in dishes like grilled seafood, grilled meats, Thai-style barbecue, and delectable desserts.

7. Khlong Toei Market: This bustling fresh market is a favorite among locals. It's a great place to immerse yourself in the authentic Thai market culture and find a wide range of fresh ingredients, including meat, seafood, fruits, vegetables, and herbs. You can also sample local street food specialties like boat noodles and spicy papaya salad.

These are just a few highlights of Bangkok's vibrant markets and street food delights. Exploring these lively venues virtually will surely give you a taste of the unique culinary experiences Bangkok has to offer. Remember to indulge in the flavors and immerse yourself in the lively atmosphere when you have the opportunity to visit in person!

Bangkok is renowned for its bustling markets and mouth-watering street food. Visit the famous

Chatuchak Weekend Market, one of the world's largest markets, to explore a maze of stalls offering everything from fashion and handicrafts to delicious street food. Don't miss trying local favorites like pad Thai, green curry, mango sticky rice, and refreshing Thai iced tea.

4. Navigating the Chao Phraya River:
The Chao Phraya River is a lifeline of Bangkok, and exploring it is a must-do experience. Take a boat ride along the river to witness the city's diverse landscapes, passing by skyscrapers, temples, and traditional wooden houses. You can also opt for a dinner cruise to enjoy a romantic evening while admiring the illuminated landmarks along the riverbanks.

Navigating the Chao Phraya River is a popular way to explore Bangkok and its surrounding areas. Here's a virtual guide to help you navigate the Chao Phraya River and make the most of your journey:

1. River Taxis: River taxis, also known as express boats, are a convenient mode of

transportation along the Chao Phraya River. These boats operate on fixed routes and make stops at various piers along the river. There are different types of river taxis, including local boats with no air conditioning and tourist boats with more comfortable seating. River taxis are a cost-effective way to travel and offer great views of the city's landmarks.

2. Chao Phraya Tourist Boat: The Chao Phraya Tourist Boat is a hop-on, hop-off boat service specifically designed for tourists. It operates on a set schedule and stops at major attractions along the river, such as the Grand Palace, Wat Arun, and Chinatown. The boat has an English-speaking guide who provides information about the landmarks. It's a convenient option for exploring the riverside attractions.

3. Long-tail Boats: For a more personalized and flexible experience, you can hire a long-tail boat. These traditional Thai boats have a long propeller shaft at the rear and can navigate

through narrow canals as well as the main river. Long-tail boats offer private tours and can take you to off-the-beaten-path areas, including the smaller canals (khlongs) that give you a glimpse of traditional Thai life.

4. Dinner Cruises: If you're looking for a unique dining experience, consider taking a dinner cruise along the Chao Phraya River. Several companies offer dinner cruises that allow you to enjoy a delicious meal while taking in the stunning views of Bangkok's landmarks illuminated at night. It's a great way to relax and soak up the city's ambiance.

5. Exploring the Riverside Attractions: Along the Chao Phraya River, you'll find numerous attractions that are worth exploring. Some of the notable landmarks include the Grand Palace, Wat Arun, Wat Pho, Asiatique The Riverfront, and the ICONSIAM shopping complex. These attractions are easily accessible from the river, and you can disembark at the respective piers to visit them.

6. Sunset Views: Watching the sunset over the Chao Phraya River is a beautiful experience. Find a comfortable spot along the riverbank or aboard a boat and witness the sky transform into a palette of colors as the sun goes down. It's a magical moment that shouldn't be missed.

The Chao Phraya River offers a unique perspective of Bangkok and provides access to some of the city's most iconic landmarks and attractions.

## Tips for Navigating Bangkok:

Navigating Bangkok can be an exciting experience, but it can also be a bit overwhelming due to the city's size and traffic. Here are some tips to help you navigate Bangkok more easily:

1. Plan your routes: Before setting out, plan your routes and identify the landmarks, attractions, or neighborhoods you want to visit. Familiarize yourself with the map of Bangkok and make

note of major roads, public transportation options, and important landmarks. This will help you navigate more efficiently.

2. Use public transportation: Bangkok has an extensive public transportation system that can help you navigate the city. The BTS Skytrain, MRT subway, and Airport Rail Link are efficient modes of transportation for getting around. They are relatively fast, reliable, and can help you avoid the city's notorious traffic congestion. Purchase a rechargeable Rabbit card or a stored value card to make traveling on public transport more convenient.

3. Consider river transportation: As mentioned earlier, the Chao Phraya River is an important transportation route in Bangkok. Take advantage of the river taxis, tourist boats, or private long-tail boats to explore riverside attractions and bypass road traffic. It's a scenic and often quicker way to get around.

4. Use ride-hailing services: Ride-hailing services like Grab and Uber (or their local counterparts) are popular in Bangkok. They offer a convenient and comfortable way to get around the city, especially if you're traveling in a group or with heavy luggage. Just make sure you have internet connectivity to access the apps and book your rides.

5. Tuk-tuks and taxis: Tuk-tuks are iconic three-wheeled vehicles that can be a fun and adventurous way to get around short distances. Negotiate the fare before hopping in, as they usually don't have meters. Taxis are also widely available, but make sure the driver uses the meter or agree on a price beforehand to avoid overcharging.

6. Be aware of traffic: Bangkok is notorious for its traffic jams, especially during peak hours. Plan your journeys accordingly, allowing extra time to reach your destination. If possible, try to avoid traveling during rush hour to minimize your time spent in traffic.

7. Stay street smart: When walking around the city, be mindful of your belongings and stay alert. Keep your valuables secure and be cautious of pickpockets, especially in crowded areas. It's also advisable to carry a map or use a navigation app on your phone to avoid getting lost.Be Mindful of Scams: Like any popular tourist destination, be cautious of scams and touts. Avoid engaging with individuals offering suspiciously cheap tours or claiming that temples or attractions are closed. Stick to reputable tour operators and follow your instincts.

8. Learn basic Thai phrases: Learning a few basic Thai phrases can be helpful when communicating with locals, especially taxi drivers or when asking for directions. Simple greetings and polite phrases go a long way in fostering positive interactions.

9. Stay hydrated and dress appropriately: Bangkok can be hot and humid, so stay hydrated by carrying a water bottle with you. Dress in lightweight and breathable clothing to stay comfortable in the tropical climate. Keep in mind that when visiting temples or certain attractions, modest attire is required, covering your shoulders and knees.Dress Code: When visiting temples, including the Grand Palace and Wat Arun, dress modestly and respectfully. Both men and women should cover their shoulders and knees. Wearing comfortable shoes is advisable as you'll be doing a fair amount of walking.

By following these tips, you'll be better equipped to navigate Bangkok and make the most of your time in this vibrant city. Enjoy your exploration of Bangkok's fascinating neighborhoods, landmarks, and cultural treasures!

# Chiang Mai

located in the mountainous region of northern Thailand, is a city renowned for its ancient temples and breathtaking landscapes. Let's explore the highlights of this culturally rich and naturally beautiful destination.

1. Temples (Wats): Chiang Mai is home to over 300 temples, known as wats, each with its own unique charm and significance. Some of the must-visit temples include Wat Phra That Doi Suthep, perched on a mountain with stunning city views; Wat Chedi Luang, featuring a towering pagoda; and Wat Phra Singh, housing a revered Buddha statue.

2. Old City: The historic center of Chiang Mai is surrounded by a moat and remnants of ancient walls. Exploring the narrow streets and alleyways of the Old City is a delightful experience, with its traditional architecture, vibrant markets, and local eateries. Don't miss the famous Sunday Walking Street, where you

can shop for handicrafts, sample local delicacies, and enjoy traditional music and dance performances.

3. Doi Suthep-Pui National Park: Just a short drive from the city, this national park offers a tranquil escape into nature. It is crowned by Doi Suthep, a mountain peak with a revered temple (Wat Phra That Doi Suthep). Besides visiting the temple, you can also enjoy hiking trails, refreshing waterfalls, and panoramic views of the surrounding landscapes.

4. Elephant Sanctuaries: Chiang Mai is known for its ethical elephant sanctuaries that provide a humane environment for these magnificent creatures. You can observe elephants in their natural habitat, learn about their conservation, and even participate in activities like feeding and bathing them. Make sure to choose a reputable sanctuary that prioritizes the welfare of the elephants.

5. Hill Tribe Villages: The region around Chiang Mai is home to several hill tribe communities, each with its distinct traditions and way of life. Visiting these villages offers a glimpse into their fascinating culture, traditional crafts, and warm hospitality. Popular tribes to visit include the Karen, Hmong, and Lisu tribes.

6. Night Bazaar: Experience the vibrant atmosphere of Chiang Mai's Night Bazaar, where you can shop for handicrafts, clothing, and souvenirs. This bustling market is an excellent place to indulge in local street food, watch cultural performances, and get a traditional Thai massage.

7. Thai Cuisine: Chiang Mai is a food lover's paradise, with a wide array of delectable dishes to try. Sample traditional Northern Thai cuisine, such as khao soi (curry noodle soup), sai ua (spicy sausage), and gaeng hang lay (Burmese-style pork curry). Don't forget to explore the local markets and street food stalls to savor the authentic flavors of the region.

Whether you're exploring the ancient temples, immersing yourself in the local culture, or enjoying the natural beauty of the surrounding landscapes, Chiang Mai offers a memorable experience that combines history, spirituality, and natural wonders.

## Exploring the historical wonders of the Old City in Chiang Mai

is a fascinating journey that takes you back in time. Here are some key attractions and experiences that showcase the city's rich history:

1. Tha Phae Gate: This imposing gate is one of the main entrances to the Old City and serves as a symbolic entrance to the historic area. Take a stroll around the gate, admire its intricate design, and imagine the bustling activity that once took place here.

2. Temples (Wats): The Old City is dotted with numerous temples, each with its own

architectural style and historical significance. Some notable temples within the Old City walls include Wat Chedi Luang, Wat Phra Singh, and Wat Chiang Man. Marvel at the intricate carvings, ornate pagodas, and revered Buddha statues found within these ancient temples.

3. Three Kings Monument: Located at the center of the Old City, the Three Kings Monument commemorates the founding of Chiang Mai. The statue represents the three kings—King Mengrai, King Ramkhamhaeng of Sukhothai, and King Ngam Muang of Phayao—who played pivotal roles in the establishment of the city.

4. City Walls and Moat: The Old City is encircled by a 700-year-old wall and a moat, which were built to protect the city from invaders. Take a leisurely walk along the wall and explore the four main gates—Tha Phae, Pratu Chiang Mai, Pratu Tha Pae, and Pratu Suan Dok. The moat offers a tranquil setting for a relaxing stroll or a boat ride.

5. Lanna Folklife Museum: Housed in a former palace, the Lanna Folklife Museum offers insights into the traditional Lanna culture of northern Thailand. Explore the exhibits showcasing traditional costumes, artifacts, tools, and everyday objects, providing a glimpse into the daily life of the people in the region.

6. Wat Phra That Doi Suthep: While not located within the Old City, a visit to Chiang Mai is incomplete without experiencing the ancient temple of Wat Phra That Doi Suthep. Situated atop Doi Suthep mountain, this sacred temple offers panoramic views of the city. Legend has it that a white elephant carried a relic of the Buddha to this site, leading to the temple's construction.

7. Walking Streets: The Old City comes alive with vibrant markets during the evenings. Don't miss the famous Sunday Walking Street, where the streets are lined with stalls selling local handicrafts, art, clothing, and street food. You

can also explore the Saturday Walking Street on Wualai Road, which offers a similar experience.

Immerse yourself in the historical charm of the Old City in Chiang Mai, where every street and structure has a story to tell. Discover the rich cultural heritage, intricate architecture, and the enduring spirit of this ancient city.

# Doi Suthep

a mountain located near Chiang Mai, is not only a natural wonder but also home to one of the most revered temples in Thailand: Wat Phra That Doi Suthep. Here's a glimpse into the magnificent Doi Suthep and its sacred secrets:

1. Legend and History: According to legend, a sacred relic of the Buddha was placed on the back of a white elephant, which was released into the jungle. The elephant climbed up Doi Suthep mountain, trumpeted three times, and then died. This was interpreted as a sign, leading to the construction of Wat Phra That Doi Suthep in 1383. The temple has since become a significant pilgrimage site for Buddhists.

2. Temple Complex: Wat Phra That Doi Suthep is an architectural masterpiece. As you ascend the stairs, you'll be greeted by a magnificent seven-headed Naga (serpent) staircase railing, believed to provide protection and ward off evil spirits. The temple complex features golden

chedis (pagodas), statues, shrines, and intricate Lanna-style architecture.

3. Phra That: The main attraction of the temple is the Phra That, a golden chedi enshrining the sacred relic of the Buddha. The chedi is believed to house holy relics and is a symbol of spiritual enlightenment. Visitors can pay respects, make offerings, and experience the spiritual ambiance surrounding this revered relic.

4. Panoramic Views: From the temple grounds, you can enjoy breathtaking panoramic views of Chiang Mai and the surrounding countryside. The beauty of the landscape, especially during sunrise or sunset, adds to the mystical allure of Doi Suthep.

5. Pilgrimage and Festivals: Wat Phra That Doi Suthep is an important site for Buddhists, who often make the pilgrimage to pay homage to the temple. During festivals such as Visakha Bucha and Loy Krathong, the temple complex is adorned with lights, decorations, and vibrant

celebrations. Witnessing these festive events can provide a deeper understanding of the local culture and religious practices.

6. Forest and Nature: Doi Suthep is part of the Doi Suthep-Pui National Park, offering opportunities for nature lovers. Explore the lush forest trails, encounter diverse flora and fauna, and visit stunning waterfalls, such as Bhubing Palace's Royal Gardens.

7. Meditation and Retreats: Some areas around Doi Suthep offer meditation retreats and centers where visitors can immerse themselves in a serene environment for self-reflection and contemplation. These retreats provide an opportunity to learn about Buddhist philosophy and meditation techniques.

Doi Suthep and Wat Phra That Doi Suthep encapsulate the spiritual and natural essence of Chiang Mai. A visit to this sacred mountain and temple complex allows you to witness the grandeur of Thai architecture, experience the devotion of pilgrims, and connect with the tranquil beauty of nature.

## Experiencing the Charm of the Sunday Night Market

The Sunday Night Market in Chiang Mai is a vibrant and bustling event that showcases the rich culture, craftsmanship, and culinary delights of the city. Here's what you can expect when experiencing the charm of the Sunday Night Market:

1. Street Market Extravaganza: The Sunday Night Market stretches along the entire length of Ratchadamnoen Road in the heart of the Old City. As the sun sets, the street transforms into a lively market filled with stalls and vendors selling a vast array of goods. From handicrafts and clothing to artwork and home decor, there is something for everyone.

2. Handicrafts and Artwork: The market is a treasure trove for handicraft enthusiasts. You'll find a wide range of traditional crafts such as intricately woven textiles, handmade ceramics, wood carvings, silverware, and colorful hill tribe products. Many of these items are produced by skilled artisans from the surrounding villages.

3. Local Delicacies: The Sunday Night Market is a haven for food lovers. The air is filled with mouth-watering aromas as food stalls line the streets, offering an array of delectable treats. Sample local specialties like khao soi (curry noodle soup), sai ua (spicy sausage), mango sticky rice, fried insects (for the adventurous), and a variety of Thai snacks and desserts. You can also find vegetarian and vegan options.

4. Cultural Performances: As you wander through the market, you may come across stages where traditional music, dance, and cultural performances take place. Watch as talented performers showcase traditional Thai dances, music, and even martial arts demonstrations.

These performances add an extra layer of charm and cultural immersion to the market experience.

5. Local Artists and Musicians: The Sunday Night Market is known for its lively atmosphere, and you'll often find local artists displaying their works or musicians entertaining the crowds. From painters and photographers to musicians and street performers, the market provides a platform for local talents to showcase their creativity.

6. Massage and Reflexology: After a long day of exploring the market, take a break and indulge in a traditional Thai massage or reflexology session. You'll find massage stalls and spas offering rejuvenating treatments to help you relax and recharge.

7. People-Watching and Atmosphere: The Sunday Night Market attracts both locals and tourists, creating a vibrant and diverse atmosphere. It's a great opportunity to observe the local way of life, interact with friendly

vendors, and immerse yourself in the lively energy of the market. Enjoy the colorful sights, sounds, and scents as you navigate through the bustling crowd.

The Sunday Night Market in Chiang Mai is a true delight for the senses. It offers a unique opportunity to explore local craftsmanship, taste authentic Thai cuisine, experience traditional performances, and soak in the vibrant ambiance of this beloved market.

**Trekking Adventures in the Surrounding Mountains**

The surrounding mountains of Chiang Mai offer fantastic opportunities for trekking adventures, allowing you to immerse yourself in the natural beauty of northern Thailand. Here's what you can expect when embarking on trekking adventures in the mountains near Chiang Mai:

1. Diverse Landscapes: The mountains around Chiang Mai boast diverse landscapes, ranging

from lush forests to cascading waterfalls and terraced rice fields. As you trek through these areas, you'll encounter breathtaking scenery, rich biodiversity, and stunning viewpoints that offer panoramic vistas.

2. Hiking Trails: There are numerous hiking trails catering to different levels of difficulty and duration. From shorter half-day treks to multi-day expeditions, you can choose an adventure that suits your preferences and fitness level. Some popular trails include Doi Suthep, Doi Inthanon (the highest peak in Thailand), and Doi Pui.

3. Hill Tribe Villages: Trekking in the mountains provides an opportunity to visit and interact with the fascinating hill tribe communities that call this region home. You can learn about their unique cultures, traditions, and way of life. The Karen, Hmong, Lisu, and Akha tribes are among the prominent ones you may encounter.

4. Homestays and Cultural Exchange: To fully immerse yourself in the local culture, consider staying overnight in a hill tribe village. Homestays offer an authentic experience, allowing you to live with a local family, participate in their daily activities, and gain insights into their traditions and customs. It's an excellent opportunity for cultural exchange and meaningful connections.

5. Waterfalls and Swimming: Many trekking routes in the mountains lead to stunning waterfalls where you can take a refreshing dip in the natural pools. Enjoy the cool mountain waters as you relax and rejuvenate amidst the serene surroundings. Popular waterfalls include Mae Sa Waterfall, Bua Thong Sticky Waterfalls, and Huay Kaew Waterfall.

6. Wildlife and Flora: The mountains of Chiang Mai are home to a diverse array of wildlife and flora. Keep an eye out for native species such as gibbons, macaques, hornbills, and various tropical birds. If you're lucky, you might catch a

glimpse of elephants or even spot elusive creatures like leopards and Asian black bears (though sightings are rare).

7. Adventure Activities: In addition to trekking, you can often combine your mountain adventure with other thrilling activities. Ziplining through the forest canopy, bamboo rafting along rivers, and off-road biking are popular options that add an extra element of excitement to your trekking experience.

When planning a trekking adventure in the surrounding mountains of Chiang Mai, it's advisable to choose a reputable tour operator or guide who prioritizes responsible and sustainable practices. They can provide necessary equipment, local expertise, and ensure your safety while minimizing the impact on the environment and local communities.

Embarking on a trekking adventure allows you to connect with nature, challenge yourself physically, and discover the hidden gems of the mountainous landscapes around Chiang Mai. It's an unforgettable experience that offers a unique perspective on the region's natural wonders.

# Phuket and the Andaman Sea

Phuket, located in the Andaman Sea in southern Thailand, is a popular destination known for its stunning beaches, crystal-clear waters, and vibrant nightlife. Here's what you can expect when exploring Phuket and the Andaman Sea:

1. Beaches: Phuket is renowned for its picturesque beaches that offer something for everyone. Patong Beach is the most well-known and bustling with activity, offering water sports, beach bars, and a lively nightlife scene. Other popular beaches include Kata Beach and Karon Beach, which are great for swimming, sunbathing, and enjoying water activities like snorkeling and surfing.

2. Island Hopping: Phuket serves as a gateway to a multitude of beautiful islands in the Andaman Sea. Take a boat tour and explore nearby islands like Phi Phi Islands, known for its stunning limestone cliffs and turquoise waters, or visit the

Similan Islands, a national park renowned for its vibrant coral reefs, marine life, and excellent diving opportunities.

3. Diving and Snorkeling: The Andaman Sea is a paradise for divers and snorkelers. With its clear waters and vibrant marine ecosystem, it offers excellent visibility and a chance to explore colorful coral reefs teeming with tropical fish, sea turtles, and even reef sharks. Popular dive sites include the Similan Islands, Koh Racha, and Koh Phi Phi.

4. Phi Phi Islands: The Phi Phi Islands, consisting of Phi Phi Don and Phi Phi Leh, are a must-visit destination. Phi Phi Leh is famous for Maya Bay, featured in the movie "The Beach," and offers stunning limestone cliffs, hidden coves, and pristine beaches. Phi Phi Don is the main island with a lively atmosphere, bars, restaurants, and various accommodation options.

5. Phang Nga Bay: Located northeast of Phuket, Phang Nga Bay is known for its towering

limestone karsts, emerald-green waters, and hidden lagoons. Explore the bay on a boat tour, kayak through the limestone caves, and visit the famous James Bond Island (Khao Phing Kan), featured in the movie "The Man with the Golden Gun."

6. Old Phuket Town: Take a break from the beach and explore the cultural and historical side of Phuket by visiting Old Phuket Town. This charming area showcases a mix of Thai, Chinese, and European influences in its architecture, colorful buildings, and vibrant street art. Stroll along the streets, visit the temples, and savor local cuisine at the bustling markets and trendy cafes.

7. Sunset Cruises: Enjoy the beauty of the Andaman Sea and its stunning sunsets on a sunset cruise. Cruise along the coast, sipping cocktails, and taking in the breathtaking views as the sun dips below the horizon.

Phuket and the Andaman Sea offer a combination of natural beauty, thrilling water activities, cultural experiences, and vibrant nightlife. Whether you seek relaxation on pristine beaches, adventure in the underwater world, or exploration of nearby islands, this region provides a diverse range of experiences for every traveller.

## Relaxing on Pristine Beaches and Island Getaways

When it comes to relaxing on pristine beaches and indulging in island getaways, Thailand offers a plethora of options. Here are some idyllic beach destinations and island getaways that are perfect for unwinding and rejuvenating:

1. Phuket: As mentioned earlier, Phuket is a popular destination known for its beautiful beaches. From lively and bustling beaches like Patong to quieter and more serene options like Kata and Karon, you can find a beach that suits

your preferences. Enjoy sunbathing, swimming, and water sports, or simply unwind with a book under the shade of palm trees.

2. Phi Phi Islands: The Phi Phi Islands, including Phi Phi Don and Phi Phi Leh, are a tropical paradise. With stunning limestone cliffs, turquoise waters, and powdery white sand beaches, these islands offer a picture-perfect setting for relaxation. Visit Maya Bay, go snorkeling, or take a leisurely boat trip around the islands.

3. Koh Lanta: Koh Lanta is a laid-back island known for its pristine beaches and tranquil atmosphere. With fewer crowds compared to some of the more popular destinations, it's an ideal spot for those seeking a peaceful beach getaway. Relax on the soft sands, enjoy swimming in the clear waters, or explore nearby islands on a boat tour.

4. Koh Samui: Located in the Gulf of Thailand, Koh Samui is a tropical paradise with

palm-fringed beaches and luxury resorts. Chaweng Beach is the most popular and bustling, while Lamai Beach offers a more relaxed ambiance. You can also explore lesser-known beaches like Bophut and Maenam for a quieter experience.

5. Krabi and Railay Beach: Krabi is famous for its stunning limestone cliffs and crystal-clear waters. Railay Beach, located on a peninsula accessible only by boat, is a must-visit destination. Surrounded by towering cliffs, Railay Beach offers a tranquil and secluded atmosphere, perfect for beach lovers and rock climbing enthusiasts.

6. Koh Chang: Situated in the eastern part of Thailand, near the border with Cambodia, Koh Chang is the second-largest island in Thailand. It boasts beautiful beaches, lush rainforests, and an abundance of marine life. Explore the pristine beaches of White Sand Beach and Klong Prao Beach, or head to the quieter and more secluded Long Beach.

7. Koh Tao: Known as a diving paradise, Koh Tao is a small island in the Gulf of Thailand. It offers clear turquoise waters, vibrant coral reefs, and an array of marine life. Besides diving, you can relax on the stunning beaches, go snorkeling, or take boat trips to nearby islands.

Whether you prefer lively beach destinations or secluded island getaways, Thailand offers a diverse range of options to suit your preferences. From well-known destinations like Phuket and Phi Phi Islands to lesser-known gems like Koh Lanta and Koh Chang, these pristine beaches and island retreats provide the perfect backdrop for relaxation and rejuvenation.

**Diving into the Underwater World of the Similan Islands**

Diving into the underwater world of the Similan Islands is an experience of a lifetime. Located in the Andaman Sea, the Similan Islands are a renowned diving destination in Thailand. Here's what you can expect when exploring the underwater wonders of the Similan Islands:

1. Pristine Coral Reefs: The Similan Islands are known for their vibrant and healthy coral reefs. The underwater landscapes are adorned with colorful coral formations, including hard and soft corals, providing a stunning backdrop for your diving adventures.

2. Marine Biodiversity: The Similan Islands are home to a rich and diverse marine ecosystem. As you dive into the crystal-clear waters, you'll encounter an abundance of marine life, including tropical fish, reef sharks, rays, moray eels, sea turtles, and even whale sharks if you're lucky. The islands are also a popular spot for manta ray sightings.

3. Dive Sites: The Similan Islands offer a range of dive sites suitable for divers of various experience levels. Each dive site has its unique features, including underwater rock formations, swim-throughs, and pinnacles. Some popular

dive sites include Elephant Head Rock, Richelieu Rock (famous for its biodiversity), and East of Eden.

4. Visibility and Water Conditions: The visibility in the waters around the Similan Islands is generally excellent, often exceeding 30 meters (100 feet). The calm and clear waters make for great diving conditions, allowing you to fully appreciate the underwater beauty and spot marine creatures from a distance.

5. Liveaboards: Many divers opt for liveaboard trips to the Similan Islands, which offer an immersive diving experience. Liveaboard trips typically include multiple dives per day, allowing you to explore different dive sites and maximize your time in the water. It's also a great way to meet fellow divers and enjoy the camaraderie of like-minded individuals.

6. Diving Courses: If you're new to diving or looking to enhance your skills, the Similan Islands offer diving courses for all levels. From

introductory Discover Scuba Diving programs to advanced certifications like PADI Open Water and beyond, you can take advantage of the professional dive centers and instructors available on the islands.

7. Natural Beauty: The Similan Islands are not just about the underwater world; they also boast stunning natural beauty above the surface. Between dives, take the opportunity to relax on the pristine white sand beaches, explore the jungle trails, and enjoy breathtaking views from the viewpoints scattered across the islands.

It's worth noting that the Similan Islands are part of a national park, and certain areas may have restrictions in place to protect the marine environment. It's important to follow responsible diving practices and adhere to guidelines set by dive operators and park authorities to ensure the conservation of this precious ecosystem.

Diving in the Similan Islands offers a unique opportunity to immerse yourself in a world of vibrant marine life, stunning coral reefs, and awe-inspiring underwater landscapes. Whether you're a seasoned diver or just starting your diving journey, exploring the underwater world of the Similan Islands will undoubtedly leave you with unforgettable memories.

# Exploring Phang Nga Bay's Stunning Limestone Karsts

Exploring Phang Nga Bay's stunning limestone karsts is a captivating experience that takes you through a unique natural landscape. Located in southern Thailand, Phang Nga Bay is known for its towering limestone cliffs, emerald-green waters, and hidden lagoons. Here's what you can expect when exploring this remarkable destination:

1. Spectacular Karst Formations: The highlight of Phang Nga Bay is undoubtedly its limestone karsts that jut out of the water, creating a dramatic and awe-inspiring sight. These

towering cliffs, covered in lush vegetation, form a stunning backdrop against the azure waters of the bay. The shapes and formations of the karsts are diverse and fascinating, with some resembling pillars, needles, or even the shape of animals.

2. James Bond Island (Khao Phing Kan): Perhaps the most famous attraction in Phang Nga Bay, James Bond Island gained its name after appearing in the 1974 James Bond movie "the film "The Man with the Golden Gun." The famous limestone karst, which appears to be floating alone in the lake, has come to represent the area..

3. Hidden Lagoons and Caves: Phang Nga Bay is also home to hidden lagoons and caves waiting to be explored. One of the most renowned is Hong Island, featuring an enclosed lagoon surrounded by limestone cliffs. Accessible only by kayak or small boat during high tide, it offers a tranquil and otherworldly experience. Additionally, there are other caves

and hongs (Thai for "room") to discover, such as Bat Cave and Diamond Cave.

4. Sea Kayaking: Exploring Phang Nga Bay by sea kayak is a popular way to navigate through the limestone karsts and explore the hidden gems of the region. Paddle through narrow channels, glide into secluded lagoons, and marvel at the unique rock formations up close. It's a peaceful and intimate way to appreciate the natural beauty of the bay.

5. Wildlife and Nature: Phang Nga Bay is not only visually stunning but also a haven for wildlife and biodiversity. Keep an eye out for the varied bird species that inhabit the area, including the white-bellied sea eagle, as well as the occasional sighting of monkeys and reptiles. The mangrove forests fringing the bay are also worth exploring, as they support a rich ecosystem and offer a chance to spot diverse flora and fauna.

6. Sunset Cruises: Witnessing the sunset over the limestone karsts of Phang Nga Bay is a truly magical experience. Consider taking a sunset cruise, where you can relax on a boat, savor the breathtaking views, and capture stunning photographs as the sun paints the sky in vibrant hues.

7. Sustainable Tourism: Phang Nga Bay is part of a national marine park, and efforts are made to preserve its natural beauty and fragile ecosystem. When visiting, choose responsible tour operators who prioritize sustainable practices, such as minimizing waste and promoting conservation.

Exploring Phang Nga Bay's stunning limestone karsts allows you to immerse yourself in a unique and mesmerizing natural environment. Whether you choose to kayak through hidden lagoons, cruise around the bay, or simply admire the dramatic cliffs from a distance, the beauty and grandeur of Phang Nga Bay will leave a lasting impression.

# Discovering the Cultural Gems of Old Phuket Town

This is a delightful experience that takes you through a rich tapestry of history, architecture, and vibrant street art. Here's what you can expect when exploring this charming part of Phuket:

1. Sino-Portuguese Architecture: Old Phuket Town is famous for its well-preserved Sino-Portuguese architecture. Walking through the streets, you'll be greeted by colorful buildings adorned with intricate details, ornate facades, and characteristic shophouse designs. The blend of Chinese and European influences creates a unique architectural style that reflects the town's rich history as a trading hub.

2. Thalang Road: Thalang Road is the main street in Old Phuket Town and the perfect starting point for your exploration. Stroll along this bustling street lined with beautifully restored

buildings, and immerse yourself in the vibrant atmosphere. You'll find an array of cafes, boutique shops, art galleries, and local eateries showcasing the town's cultural diversity.

3. Chinese Shrines and Temples: Phuket has a significant Chinese community, and Old Phuket Town is home to several Chinese shrines and temples. Explore the ornate interiors of these places of worship, adorned with intricate woodwork, colorful murals, and traditional Chinese motifs. Notable temples include Jui Tui Shrine and Put Jaw Chinese Temple.

4. Baba-Nyonya Heritage Museum: Delve into the fascinating history of the Peranakan Chinese community, also known as Baba-Nyonya, at the Baba-Nyonya Heritage Museum. This restored townhouse showcases the lifestyle, traditions, and heritage of the Peranakan people through its meticulously recreated rooms and displays of antiques and artifacts.

5. Street Art and Murals: Old Phuket Town has transformed into an open-air art gallery with its vibrant street art and murals. As you wander through the streets, keep an eye out for colorful paintings and murals depicting local culture, history, and Phuket's unique charm. The street art adds a modern and creative touch to the traditional surroundings.

6. Sunday Walking Street Market: The Sunday Walking Street Market is a must-visit event in Old Phuket Town. Every Sunday evening, Thalang Road transforms into a lively market where vendors sell an array of goods, including local handicrafts, clothing, street food, and souvenirs. It's a fantastic opportunity to immerse yourself in the local culture, indulge in delicious street food, and shop for unique treasures.

7. Old Phuket Town Art and Cultural Festival: If you happen to visit during the Old Phuket Town Art and Cultural Festival, you're in for a treat. This annual event celebrates the town's cultural heritage through a series of performances,

exhibitions, and activities. It's a vibrant and colorful celebration that showcases the best of Old Phuket Town's arts, culture, and traditions.

Old Phuket Town offers a captivating blend of history, culture, and creativity. Exploring its charming streets, admiring the unique architecture, and immersing yourself in the local arts scene will give you a deeper understanding and appreciation of Phuket's cultural heritage.

**Northern Treasures:**
The northern region of Thailand is known for its stunning landscapes, rich cultural heritage, and unique attractions. In this journey through northern treasures, we will explore Chiang Rai, Pai, and other notable destinations beyond.

# Chiang Rai:

Chiang Rai is a charming city located in the northernmost part of Thailand. It is renowned for its extensive cultural heritage, magnificent temples, and breathtaking scenery.. Here are some highlights of Chiang Rai:

1. White Temple (Wat Rong Khun): The White Temple is a must-visit attraction in Chiang Rai. It is a contemporary Buddhist temple known for its striking white exterior adorned with intricate carvings. The temple's design is unique and incorporates elements of traditional Thai art with modern influences.

2. Blue Temple (Wat Rong Suea Ten): Another noteworthy temple in Chiang Rai is the Blue Temple. Its vibrant blue color, elaborate decorations, and beautiful murals make it a sight to behold. The temple exudes a serene atmosphere and is a popular spot for locals and tourists alike.

3. Chiang Rai Night Bazaar: The Night Bazaar in Chiang Rai is a bustling market where you can find a wide range of goods, including local handicrafts, clothing, souvenirs, and delicious street food. It's a great place to immerse yourself in the local culture, try authentic Thai dishes, and shop for unique items.

4. Hill Tribe Villages: Chiang Rai is surrounded by several hill tribe villages, where you can experience the unique cultures and traditions of the local ethnic groups. The Akha, Karen, and Hmong tribes are among the communities you can visit. It's an opportunity to learn about their way of life, witness traditional crafts, and interact with the friendly locals.

5. Golden Triangle: Chiang Rai is close to the Golden Triangle, a historically significant area where Thailand, Laos, and Myanmar meet. You can take a boat trip along the Mekong River to explore the region and enjoy the scenic views. The Golden Triangle was once notorious for its opium trade, and you can learn about its history at the Hall of Opium museum.

6. Doi Tung: Located near Chiang Rai, Doi Tung is a mountainous area famous for its beautiful gardens and the Doi Tung Development Project. The project focuses on sustainable development and improving the lives of local communities. You can visit the Mae Fah Luang Gardens, which showcase a variety of flowers and plants, and explore the Royal Villa, a former residence of the late Princess Mother.

Chiang Rai offers a blend of cultural experiences, natural beauty, and unique attractions. Whether you're exploring the magnificent temples, immersing yourself in the local markets, or delving into the history of the Golden Triangle, Chiang Rai is sure to captivate you with its charm and beauty.

**Golden Triangle**:
A short drive from Chiang Rai will take you to the Golden Triangle, where Thailand, Laos, and Myanmar meet. This historically significant area was once notorious for its opium trade. Nowadays, it offers scenic views of the Mekong River and the opportunity to explore the Hall of Opium, a museum that delves into the region's drug history.

The Golden Triangle is a region located in the northern part of Thailand where the borders of Thailand, Laos, and Myanmar converge. It is named after the shape formed by the Mekong River, which runs through the area. Here's what you need to know about the Golden Triangle:

1. Opium Trade History: The Golden Triangle was historically notorious for its opium trade. The region was a major producer of opium, and the trade flourished in the 20th century. Opium

poppy cultivation has significantly reduced in recent years due to government initiatives and alternative crop programs.

2. Scenic Beauty: The Golden Triangle offers stunning natural beauty and picturesque landscapes. The Mekong River, flanked by lush green mountains, forms a breathtaking backdrop. You can enjoy boat trips along the river, taking in the scenic views and exploring the surrounding areas.

3. Hall of Opium Museum: Located in the Golden Triangle, the Hall of Opium is a museum dedicated to educating visitors about the history and impact of the opium trade. It provides insights into the cultivation, production, and distribution of opium, as well as the efforts to combat drug trafficking. The museum features interactive exhibits, multimedia presentations, and historical artefacts.

4. Border Towns and Crossings: In the Golden Triangle, you'll find several border towns and

crossings that allow you to easily visit neighboring countries. For example, you can cross the river into Laos and explore towns such as Huay Xai or take a boat ride to the small town of Chiang Saen in Thailand. These crossings provide opportunities to experience different cultures, cuisines, and traditions.

5. River Cruises: One of the popular activities in the Golden Triangle is taking a river cruise along the Mekong River. You can embark on a scenic boat trip, witnessing the confluence of the three countries and enjoying the tranquil surroundings. River cruises often include stops at local villages and attractions along the way.

6. Ethnic Diversity: The Golden Triangle region is home to various ethnic groups and hill tribes, such as the Akha, Lisu, and Yao. You can visit their villages, interact with the locals, and learn about their traditional customs and way of life. It's a chance to gain insights into the cultural diversity of the region.

Visiting the Golden Triangle allows you to explore the historical significance, natural beauty, and cultural diversity of this unique border region. Whether you're interested in the opium trade history, enjoying river cruises, or experiencing the local cultures, the Golden Triangle offers a fascinating and enriching experience.

# Doi Tung:

Doi Tung is a mountain located near Chiang Rai, offering a cooler climate and lush greenery. The Doi Tung Development Project has transformed the area, providing sustainable livelihoods for local communities and preserving the environment. Don't miss the beautiful Mae Fah Luang Gardens, which display a variety of plants and flowers. The Royal Villa, a former residence of the late Princess Mother, showcases traditional Lanna architecture.

Doi Tung is a mountain located in the Mae Fah Luang District of Chiang Rai Province,

Thailand. It is part of the Doi Tung Development Project, a royal initiative aimed at improving the lives of local communities and preserving the environment. Here's what you need to know about Doi Tung:

1. Mae Fah Luang Gardens: At the heart of Doi Tung is the Mae Fah Luang Gardens, a beautiful botanical garden that showcases a variety of flowers, plants, and trees. The gardens are meticulously landscaped and offer stunning views of the surrounding mountains. You can explore different themed gardens, including the Thai-style garden, the Italian-style garden, and the vibrant flower gardens.

2. Royal Villa: Adjacent to the Mae Fah Luang Gardens is the Royal Villa, also known as the Doi Tung Palace. This was the former residence of the late Princess Mother, Somdej Phra Srinagarindra. The villa is an excellent example of traditional Lanna architecture and is open to the public as a museum. You can explore the various rooms and see the personal belongings

of the Princess Mother while enjoying the scenic views from the villa's terrace.

3. Doi Tung Development Project: The Doi Tung Development Project was initiated to promote sustainable development and improve the lives of local hill tribe communities. The project focuses on creating alternative livelihoods for opium poppy growers by introducing agricultural practices, vocational training, and handicraft production. Visitors can learn about these initiatives and support the local communities by purchasing handicrafts and products made by the hill tribes.

4. Akha and Yao Hill Tribe Villages: Doi Tung is home to several hill tribe villages, including Akha and Yao communities. You can visit these villages to gain insights into their traditional way of life, customs, and craftsmanship. Engaging with the locals allows you to understand their cultural heritage and appreciate their unique traditions.

5. Doi Tung Viewpoint: To appreciate the stunning panoramic views of the surrounding landscape, head to the Doi Tung Viewpoint. Located on the peak of Doi Tung, it offers sweeping vistas of the mountains, valleys, and forests. The viewpoint is an ideal spot to enjoy the beauty of the region and take memorable photographs.

Doi Tung is not only a scenic mountain but also a testament to sustainable development and community empowerment. Exploring the Mae Fah Luang Gardens, visiting the Royal Villa, and engaging with the local hill tribe communities provide an enriching and meaningful experience that highlights the beauty and positive impact of the Doi Tung Development Project.

## Mae Sai:

Mae Sai is a border town between Thailand and Myanmar, known for its bustling markets. Take a stroll through the vibrant streets and explore the local shops selling a range of goods, including handicrafts, gems, and textiles. For a unique experience, you can even cross the border into Myanmar for a short visit to the town of Tachileik, where you can experience a different culture and cuisine.

Mae Sai is a border town located in the northernmost part of Thailand, in Chiang Rai Province. Situated on the border with Myanmar, Mae Sai offers a unique cultural and commercial experience. Here's what you need to know about Mae Sai:

1. Mae Sai Market: The bustling Mae Sai Market is a major attraction in the town. It is a vibrant hub of activity where you can find a wide range of goods, including clothing, accessories, electronics, and local handicrafts. The market is known for its gemstones and jewelry, and you can find a variety of precious and semi-precious stones. It's a great place to shop for souvenirs and experience the local atmosphere.

2. Tachileik, Myanmar: Mae Sai is the main border crossing point between Thailand and Myanmar. By crossing the border bridge, you can enter the town of Tachileik on the Myanmar side. Tachileik offers a different cultural experience, and you can explore its markets, temples, and local cuisine. Remember to check the visa requirements and border regulations before planning a visit across the border.

3. Wat Phra That Doi Wao: Perched on a hill overlooking Mae Sai, Wat Phra That Doi Wao is a temple that offers panoramic views of the town and the surrounding countryside. The temple features a golden chedi (stupa) and a large Buddha statue. It is a serene and peaceful place for contemplation and photography.

4. Mae Sai Riverfront: The Mae Sai Riverfront area is a pleasant place to take a leisurely stroll along the banks of the Sai River. You can enjoy views of the river and the bustling trade activities between Thailand and Myanmar. There are also restaurants and cafes where you can

relax and savor local delicacies while watching the river flow.

5. Border Gate and Friendship Bridge: The Mae Sai Border Gate and the Friendship Bridge are significant landmarks in the town. These are the points where travelers can cross the border between Thailand and Myanmar. The Friendship Bridge, spanning the Sai River, symbolizes the connection and friendship between the two nations.

6. Doi Wao Forest Park: Located near Mae Sai, Doi Wao Forest Park is a peaceful nature reserve that offers scenic views and hiking trails. It is known for its lush vegetation, including various species of orchids and ferns. The park is an excellent place for nature enthusiasts and offers opportunities for birdwatching and relaxation amidst nature.

Mae Sai is a vibrant town that offers a glimpse into cross-border trade and cultural diversity. Whether you're exploring the bustling markets, crossing the border into Myanmar, or enjoying the natural beauty of the surroundings, Mae Sai provides a unique experience at the northernmost border of Thailand.

# Pai:

Pai is a picturesque town nestled in a valley, surrounded by mountains and waterfalls. It's a popular destination for travellers seeking a laid-back atmosphere and natural beauty. Explore the Pai Canyon, a network of narrow ridges and ravines that offers breathtaking views. Visit the hot springs for a relaxing soak, and don't miss the Pai Walking Street, where you can sample local delicacies and shop for souvenirs.

Pai is a picturesque town nestled in a valley in the Mae Hong Son Province of northern Thailand. Known for its laid-back atmosphere, natural beauty, and cultural charm, Pai has become a popular destination for travelers seeking a tranquil retreat. Here's what you need to know about Pai:

1. Pai Canyon: Pai Canyon is a must-visit attraction offering stunning panoramic views of the surrounding landscapes. The canyon features narrow and winding paths, which you can explore while enjoying the breathtaking views of the valleys, mountains, and lush greenery. It's particularly beautiful during sunrise and sunset.

2. Hot Springs: Pai is known for its natural hot springs, which are perfect for relaxation and rejuvenation. Pamper yourself by soaking in the warm mineral-rich waters, which are believed to have healing properties. Some popular hot springs in the area include the Sai Ngam Hot Springs and the Tha Pai Hot Springs.

3. Walking Street: Pai Walking Street is a vibrant market that comes alive in the evenings. Here, you can find an array of local street food, handicrafts, clothing, and souvenirs. The street is lined with shops and stalls offering a diverse range of items, and it's a great place to

experience the local cuisine and immerse yourself in the lively atmosphere.

4. Pai Historical Bridge (Saphan Mae Yen): The Pai Historical Bridge, also known as the Memorial Bridge or Saphan Mae Yen, is a suspension bridge that holds historical significance. It was originally constructed during World War II by the Japanese army. Today, it serves as a pedestrian bridge and offers a picturesque view of the Pai River.

5. Waterfalls: Pai is surrounded by several beautiful waterfalls, providing opportunities for nature lovers and adventure enthusiasts. Mo Paeng Waterfall is a popular choice, where you can take a refreshing dip in the cascading pools. Pam Bok Waterfall and Mae Yen Waterfall are also worth exploring for their scenic beauty and tranquil ambiance.

6. Pai Canyon Pai Land Split: In addition to Pai Canyon, another interesting attraction is the Pai Land Split. It is a unique natural phenomenon

where the ground split open in 2008, causing a large crack. The owner of the land has turned it into a tourist spot, offering fresh fruit and homemade treats while visitors explore the area.

7. Temples: Pai is home to several beautiful temples that reflect the local culture and spiritual traditions. Wat Phra That Mae Yen is a hilltop temple offering panoramic views of Pai. Wat Nam Hu is known for its intricate carvings, and Wat Luang is the oldest temple in the area, dating back to 1831.

Pai's serene atmosphere, natural landscapes, and cultural attractions make it a delightful place to unwind and enjoy the beauty of northern Thailand. Whether you're exploring the Pai Canyon, relaxing in the hot springs, or immersing yourself in the vibrant markets, Pai offers a unique and memorable experience.

# Mae Hong Son:

Mae Hong Son is a province in northern Thailand known for its stunning natural landscapes, rich cultural heritage, and ethnic diversity. Nestled in the mountains, Mae Hong Son offers a peaceful and scenic retreat. Here's what you need to know about Mae Hong Son:

1. Pai: While Pai is a town in its own right, it is worth mentioning again as it is a popular destination within Mae Hong Son. Pai is known for its laid-back atmosphere, hot springs, waterfalls, and scenic beauty. It's a great place to relax, explore nature, and enjoy the local culture.

2. Mae Hong Son Loop: The Mae Hong Son Loop is a famous scenic route that takes you on a journey through the beautiful countryside of Mae Hong Son. This loop is a popular route for motorcyclists and road trippers, as it passes through lush forests, mountains, villages, and stunning viewpoints.

3. Mae Hong Son Town: The provincial capital, Mae Hong Son Town, offers a mix of traditional Thai and Burmese influences. The town is known for its temples, including Wat Phra That Doi Kong Mu, which offers panoramic views of the town and surrounding areas. The town's market is also worth exploring for local handicrafts, fresh produce, and delicious street food.

4. Long Neck Karen Villages: Mae Hong Son is home to several hill tribe communities, including the Long Neck Karen tribe. These tribes are known for the women who wear brass rings around their necks, giving them the appearance of elongated necks. Visiting these villages provides an opportunity to learn about their culture, traditions, and craftsmanship.

5. Tham Lod Cave: Tham Lod Cave is a spectacular cave system located in the Soppong district of Mae Hong Son. The cave features limestone formations, stalactites, and stalagmites, as well as a river flowing through it.

You can explore the cave by boat, and marvel at the unique rock formations and ancient cave paintings.

6. Doi Inthanon National Park: While Doi Inthanon National Park is located mainly in Chiang Mai Province, a portion of it stretches into Mae Hong Son. Doi Inthanon is the highest mountain in Thailand and offers beautiful hiking trails, waterfalls, and viewpoints. The park is known for its diverse flora and fauna, and it's a great place for nature lovers and adventure enthusiasts.

7. Pha Sua Waterfall: Pha Sua Waterfall is a magnificent waterfall located in Mae Sariang District. It cascades down a series of terraces, surrounded by lush greenery. The waterfall is particularly impressive during the rainy season when the water flow is at its peak.

Mae Hong Son offers a tranquil escape with its natural beauty, cultural experiences, and outdoor adventures. Whether you're exploring the towns and markets, visiting hill tribe villages, or immersing yourself in the breathtaking landscapes, Mae Hong Son promises an enriching and memorable journey.

Further west from Pai lies Mae Hong Son, a tranquil town known for its misty mountains and serene temples. The Wat Phra That Doi Kong Mu is perched on a hill and provides panoramic views of the surrounding area. Take a boat ride on the picturesque Pai River, visit the Tham Pla Fish Cave, or enjoy a rejuvenating soak in the Pong Dueat Hot Springs.

## Other Beyond Destinations:

If you have more time, consider visiting other destinations beyond Chiang Rai and Pai. Chiang Mai, the cultural hub of the north, offers a plethora of temples, night markets, and traditional performances. The Doi Inthanon National Park boasts Thailand's highest peak and stunning waterfalls.

The city of Lampang is known for its horse-drawn carriages and well-preserved Lanna architecture.

Northern Thailand is a treasure trove of natural beauty, cultural wonders, and warm hospitality. Whether you explore the temples of Chiang Rai, embrace the tranquility of Pai, or venture further into the region, your journey through these northern treasures will be an unforgettable experience.

## Uncovering the Mysteries of the White Temple (Wat Rong Khun)

The White Temple, also known as Wat Rong Khun, is a renowned Buddhist temple located in Chiang Rai, Thailand. It was designed and built by the Thai artist Chalermchai Kositpipat, who wanted to create a unique and contemporary interpretation of a Buddhist temple. The temple's construction began in 1997 and is still an ongoing project.

Here are some of the intriguing aspects and mysteries surrounding the White Temple:

1. Symbolism and Design: The White Temple is filled with intricate details and symbolic elements. The entire structure is painted white to represent the purity of the Buddha, and the fragments of mirrored glass embedded in the plaster symbolize wisdom and the Buddha's teachings reflecting throughout the world.

2. Unorthodox Elements: The temple's design deviates from traditional Buddhist architecture, incorporating various unconventional elements. For example, you will find pop culture references and contemporary icons alongside traditional Buddhist motifs, creating a unique blend of ancient and modern symbolism.

3. Bridge of the Cycle of Rebirth: One of the most captivating features of the temple is the

Bridge of the Cycle of Rebirth. The bridge is lined with outreaching hands representing desire and greed, and skulls symbolizing the transitory nature of life. Crossing the bridge is said to symbolize the journey from the cycle of rebirth to enlightenment.

4. Murals Depicting Contemporary Events: Inside the main ordination hall, you will find intricate murals that depict a mix of traditional Buddhist stories and modern-day events. These murals often feature figures like Batman, Superman, and even political leaders. The combination of these elements sparks curiosity and provokes contemplation.

5. The Mystical Golden Building: Adjacent to the White Temple, there is a golden building known as the Golden Building or the Golden Toilet. Its design is just as captivating as the White Temple itself. Visitors can go inside and observe the luxurious golden interior adorned with ornate details.

6. Spiritual Significance: The White Temple is not only a tourist attraction but also a place of spiritual significance. It serves as a place of worship and meditation for practicing Buddhists. The temple's unique design and symbolism aim to inspire reflection, contemplation, and a deeper understanding of Buddhist teachings.

While the White Temple has garnered attention and admiration from people worldwide, it is essential to note that some of the mysteries and artistic choices are subjective interpretations by the temple's creator, Chalermchai Kositpipat. Nevertheless, it continues to captivate visitors with its beauty, symbolism, and enigmatic elements.

# Hill Tribe Encounters and Cultural Immersion

Thailand is home to several indigenous ethnic groups known as hill tribes. These tribes have distinct cultures, languages, and traditions that have been preserved for generations. For travelers seeking cultural immersion and authentic experiences, encountering and learning about the hill tribes can be a fascinating and enriching journey. Here are some key points to consider:

1. Hill Tribe Diversity: Thailand is home to several hill tribe groups, including the Akha, Karen, Lisu, Hmong, Lahu, and others. Each tribe has its own unique customs, clothing, beliefs, and practices. Exploring these tribes offers an opportunity to witness the rich diversity of indigenous cultures in Thailand.

2. Locations and Access: Hill tribe villages can be found in various regions of Thailand, predominantly in the northern part of the country, including Chiang Mai, Chiang Rai, and Mae Hong Son provinces. Some tribes also reside in neighboring countries such as Myanmar, Laos, and China. Many villages are situated in remote areas, requiring some effort to reach them.

3. Cultural Sensitivity: When visiting hill tribe communities, it's crucial to approach with respect and cultural sensitivity. These tribes have faced challenges related to cultural preservation and human rights, so it's important to engage in responsible tourism practices. Seek permission before taking photographs, respect local customs and traditions, and be mindful of the impact you have on the community.

4. Homestays and Trekking: To immerse yourself in the hill tribe culture, consider staying in a homestay within a village. Homestays offer the opportunity to live with a local family, participate in their daily activities, and gain a deeper understanding of their way of life. Trekking is also popular in these regions, allowing you to explore the beautiful landscapes while interacting with hill tribe communities along the way.

5. Traditional Crafts and Artwork: Hill tribe communities are known for their craftsmanship and traditional artwork. Each tribe has its unique

handicrafts, such as intricate embroidery, weaving, silverwork, and wood carving. You can observe the artisans at work, learn about their techniques, and even purchase their handmade products as souvenirs.

6. Festivals and Celebrations: Hill tribes celebrate various festivals throughout the year, offering an opportunity to witness their vibrant traditions. Festivals often involve colorful costumes, music, dance, and traditional rituals. If you have the chance, attending a festival can be a memorable way to experience the cultural richness of the hill tribes.

7. Guided Tours and Responsible Operators: Engaging with a responsible tour operator or a local guide who has established relationships with the hill tribe communities is recommended. They can provide valuable insights, ensure respectful interactions, and help support sustainable tourism practices that benefit the tribes and the local economy.

Remember that cultural immersion is a privilege, and it is essential to approach these experiences with an open mind, curiosity, and respect for the local communities and their way of life. By engaging in responsible and ethical tourism practices, you can contribute to the preservation of the hill tribe cultures and foster mutual understanding between different cultures.

## Adventurous Explorations in Pai's Natural Beauty

Pai, a small town nestled in the mountains of northern Thailand, is renowned for its stunning natural beauty. Surrounded by lush forests, waterfalls, hot springs, and picturesque landscapes, it offers a plethora of adventurous explorations for nature enthusiasts. Here are some exciting activities to experience in Pai:

1. Waterfall Hopping: Pai is home to several beautiful waterfalls that are worth exploring. Pam Bok Waterfall, Mo Paeng Waterfall, and Mae Yen Waterfall are among the popular

choices. You can hike through the trails, swim in the refreshing pools, and marvel at the cascading waters amidst the scenic surroundings.

2. Pai Canyon: Known for its dramatic cliffs and narrow ridges, Pai Canyon offers breathtaking panoramic views of the surrounding countryside. Take a leisurely hike along the canyon's trails, cross the wooden walkways, and witness the stunning sunset vistas.

3. Hot Springs: Relax and unwind in the natural hot springs scattered around Pai. The Sai Ngam Hot Spring and Tha Pai Hot Spring are popular choices where you can soak in the therapeutic mineral-rich waters amidst the tranquil ambiance of nature.

4. Explore the Pai River: Embark on a bamboo rafting or kayaking adventure along the Pai River. Enjoy the serene and picturesque views as you paddle through the calm waters, passing by lush vegetation and mountains.

5. Trekking and Mountain Biking: The surrounding mountains and forests offer excellent opportunities for trekking and mountain biking. Join guided tours or rent a bike to explore the scenic trails, visit hill tribe villages, and immerse yourself in the natural beauty of Pai's countryside.

6. Pai Strawberry Farm: Visit the strawberry farms in Pai, where you can pick fresh strawberries during the harvesting season (usually December to February). It's a delightful experience to indulge in strawberry picking while enjoying the cool mountain air.

7. Pai Land Split: The Pai Land Split is an intriguing natural phenomenon where the ground cracked due to an earthquake in 2008. Explore the fissures, taste locally grown fruits, and learn about the resilience of the local community in overcoming the challenges caused by the event.

8. Pai Night Market: In the evenings, immerse yourself in the vibrant atmosphere of Pai's Night

Market. Sample local delicacies, shop for handmade crafts and souvenirs, and enjoy live music performances.

Remember to respect the natural environment and follow responsible tourism practices while exploring Pai's natural beauty. Leave no trace, adhere to trail etiquettes, and support local businesses and initiatives that promote sustainability and conservation. Enjoy your adventurous explorations in the breathtaking landscapes of Pai!

## Golden Triangle: Where Three Countries Converge

The Golden Triangle is a region located in Southeast Asia where the borders of three countries converge: Thailand, Laos, and Myanmar (Burma). It is named after the shape formed by the Mekong River, which acts as a natural boundary between these countries. The area is known for its historical significance, cultural diversity, and illicit drug trade history.

Here are some key points about the Golden Triangle:

1. Geographical Location: The Golden Triangle is situated in the mountainous region of mainland Southeast Asia, where the borders of Thailand, Laos, and Myanmar meet. The Mekong River serves as a significant landmark in this area.

2. Historical Significance: The Golden Triangle has a rich history and was once a major opium-producing region. In the past, the opium trade flourished here, fueling conflicts, illicit activities, and geopolitical struggles. Today, the region has undergone significant changes, and efforts have been made to shift towards legitimate industries such as tourism and agriculture.

3. Cultural Diversity: The Golden Triangle is home to various ethnic groups and hill tribes, including the Akha, Lisu, Karen, and Hmong, among others. Each tribe has its unique customs,

languages, and traditional practices. Exploring the local villages and engaging with the indigenous communities offers insights into their cultures and ways of life.

4. Tourist Attractions: The Golden Triangle has become a popular tourist destination due to its scenic landscapes and cultural attractions. Visitors can explore temples, visit local markets, take boat trips along the Mekong River, and enjoy stunning views of the surrounding mountains.

5. Opium Museum: Located in the town of Chiang Saen in Thailand, the Opium Museum provides an educational insight into the history of the opium trade in the region. The museum displays exhibits related to opium production, drug addiction, and the efforts to combat the illicit drug trade.

6. River Cruises: Taking a boat trip along the Mekong River is a popular activity in the Golden Triangle. Cruises allow visitors to enjoy the

scenic beauty of the river, observe the local way of life along its banks, and visit nearby attractions like the Hall of Opium Museum and the Golden Buddha at Wat Chedi Luang.

7. Border Crossings: The Golden Triangle offers the opportunity to visit multiple countries in a short span of time. Border crossings are possible between Thailand, Laos, and Myanmar, allowing travelers to experience the distinct cultures and landscapes of each country.

It's important to note that while the Golden Triangle has a complex history related to the drug trade, the region has transformed significantly over the years. Today, it offers visitors a chance to explore the unique blend of cultures, natural beauty, and historical sites found at the convergence of three countries.

# Ayutthaya

located in present-day Thailand, was once the capital of the Kingdom of Ayutthaya, which thrived from the 14th to the 18th century. The city was a center of trade, culture, and political power in Southeast Asia, attracting merchants, diplomats, and scholars from around the world. Today, Ayutthaya is a UNESCO World Heritage Site and a popular destination for tourists interested in exploring the ruins of this lost kingdom.

Exploring the ancient city of Ayutthaya is like embarking on a journey through time. The ruins scattered across the area provide a glimpse into the grandeur and sophistication of the past. Magnificent temples, towering prang (reliquary towers), and intricately carved statues are among the highlights of Ayutthaya's historical marvels.

One of the most famous landmarks in Ayutthaya is Wat Mahathat, known for its iconic Buddha head engulfed by the roots of a banyan tree. This captivating sight has become an iconic image of Ayutthaya and draws visitors from far and wide. Another notable temple is Wat Phra Si Sanphet, which was once the royal chapel and houses three stunning chedis (stupas) that served as the resting places for Ayutthaya kings.

Exploring Ayutthaya can be done on foot, by bicycle, or by taking a leisurely boat ride along the Chao Phraya River. As you wander through the ruins, you'll encounter historical sites at every turn. Some of the other noteworthy temples include Wat Lokayasutharam, home to a massive reclining Buddha statue, and Wat Ratchaburana, where you can descend into underground chambers and marvel at ancient murals.

Apart from its temples, Ayutthaya also offers a glimpse into the city's vibrant past through its historical sites and museums. The Ayutthaya Historical Park, covering the central part of the city, is a treasure trove of ancient ruins and well-preserved structures. The Chao Sam Phraya

National Museum houses an impressive collection of artifacts discovered in the region, providing further insights into the history and culture of Ayutthaya.

While Ayutthaya was once a bustling city, it fell into decline and was eventually abandoned due to wars and conflicts. The city was sacked and destroyed by the Burmese in the 18th century, but its legacy lives on through its ruins. Exploring Ayutthaya allows visitors to appreciate the rich heritage of Thailand and immerse themselves in the stories of a lost kingdom.

Whether you're a history enthusiast, an architecture lover, or simply curious about ancient civilizations, Ayutthaya offers a unique and captivating experience. Its ruins and historical marvels provide a window into the past, allowing visitors to connect with the grandeur and splendor of a bygone era.

# Sukhothai

known as the "Cradle of Thai Civilization," is another ancient city in Thailand that played a significant role in shaping the country's history and culture. Located in the northern part of the country, Sukhothai was the capital of the Kingdom of Sukhothai, which flourished from the 13th to the 15th century. Today, it is a UNESCO World Heritage Site and a popular destination for those seeking to explore Thailand's rich historical heritage.

The Kingdom of Sukhothai is considered the birthplace of Thai civilization, and its influence can still be seen throughout the country today. The ruins of the ancient city provide a glimpse into the glory days of the kingdom, with its remarkable architecture, stunning temples, and intricate sculptures.

One of the most iconic and well-preserved sites in Sukhothai is the Sukhothai Historical Park. This vast complex is home to numerous temples, royal palaces, and monuments that showcase the architectural and artistic achievements of the time. The park is divided into several zones, each containing its own set of ruins and attractions.

Within the Sukhothai Historical Park, Wat Mahathat is a must-visit temple. It features a large central stupa surrounded by smaller stupas and intricate Buddha statues. Wat Si Sawai is another significant temple, characterized by its three Khmer-style prangs (towers). These temples, along with many others within the park, reflect a blend of Khmer and Thai architectural styles.

Exploring Sukhothai on foot or by bicycle is a popular choice, allowing visitors to wander among the ruins at their own pace. The park is adorned with lush greenery and tranquil ponds, creating a serene and picturesque setting. It's a place where you can truly immerse yourself in the historical ambiance and appreciate the artistry and craftsmanship of ancient Thai civilization.

Apart from the Sukhothai Historical Park, there are other noteworthy sites in the surrounding area. Wat Sri Chum is a temple located just outside the park's boundaries, famous for its massive seated Buddha statue. The Ramkhamhaeng National Museum is another place of interest, exhibiting artifacts and historical objects that shed light on the kingdom's history and culture.

In addition to its architectural wonders, Sukhothai offers visitors a chance to witness traditional Thai customs and arts. The annual Loy Krathong festival, celebrated in November, is particularly vibrant in Sukhothai. During this festival, thousands of decorative floats, known as krathongs, are launched on the nearby Yom River, creating a mesmerizing spectacle of lights and colors.

Sukhothai, the Cradle of Thai Civilization, is a captivating destination for history enthusiasts, culture lovers, and anyone seeking a deeper understanding of Thailand's roots. Its ancient ruins and historical sites transport visitors back in time, allowing them to appreciate the significance of Sukhothai in shaping the country's identity and heritage.

# Lopburi

a city located in central Thailand, is famous for its unique combination of ancient temples and its resident population of monkeys. This intriguing blend of history and wildlife makes Lopburi a fascinating destination for travelers seeking a distinctive experience.

The city of Lopburi has a rich historical heritage dating back to the Dvaravati and Khmer periods. It flourished as an important center of power during the reign of the Khmer Empire and later became an influential city during the Ayutthaya

Kingdom. Today, remnants of these ancient civilizations can be seen in the form of well-preserved temples and architectural wonders.

One of the most prominent temples in Lopburi is Phra Prang Sam Yot, also known as the Monkey Temple. This Khmer-style temple features three towering prangs and is a popular attraction due to its resident macaque monkey population. The monkeys have become an integral part of the temple's charm and have free reign over the complex, often entertaining visitors with their playful antics.

Another significant temple is Wat Phra Sri Rattana Mahathat, also known as Wat Phra Kaew. This temple houses a revered Buddha image and showcases exquisite Khmer and Ayutthaya-style architecture. The temple complex is adorned with intricate carvings and sculptures, offering visitors a glimpse into the artistic achievements of the past.

While exploring the temples of Lopburi, it's common to encounter groups of monkeys roaming around the city. The monkeys have become a symbol of Lopburi and are believed to bring good fortune. However, it's important to exercise caution when interacting with them, as they can be mischievous and sometimes snatch food or belongings.

Lopburi's Monkey Festival, held annually in November, is a testament to the city's unique relationship with its primate inhabitants. During this festival, the local community offers a grand feast to the monkeys as a gesture of gratitude and respect. The event attracts both locals and tourists who come to witness the lively spectacle.

Aside from the monkeys and temples, Lopburi has other points of interest worth exploring. The Narai Ratchaniwet Palace, also known as the Summer Palace, was built during the reign of King Narai of Ayutthaya and features a blend of Thai and European architectural styles. The

Lopburi National Museum is another place to visit, housing a collection of artifacts and exhibits that provide insights into the city's history.

Visiting Lopburi offers a unique opportunity to delve into Thailand's history, marvel at ancient temples, and witness the playful interactions between humans and monkeys. The city's cultural heritage combined with the fascinating presence of its primate residents creates an unforgettable experience for travelers seeking something out of the ordinary.

## Khao Sok National Park

is indeed a remarkable ecological paradise located in southern Thailand. Spanning an area of approximately 739 square kilometers (285 square miles), it is one of the oldest and most diverse rainforests in the world, even older than the Amazon rainforest. The park is renowned for its lush greenery, towering limestone mountains, pristine lakes, and diverse wildlife, making it a haven for nature enthusiasts and eco-tourists.

One of the key features of Khao Sok National Park is its ancient rainforest, which dates back around 160 million years. This makes it older than the Amazon rainforest, which is around 55 million years old. The park is characterized by dense vegetation, including towering trees, ferns, mosses, and orchids, creating a breathtaking and immersive natural environment.

The park is home to an astonishing variety of plant and animal species, many of which are rare and endangered. You can find more than 5% of the world's animal species residing within its boundaries. Some of the notable wildlife species found in Khao Sok include Asian elephants, Malayan tapirs, clouded leopards, gibbons, macaques, and numerous bird species. The park also boasts a diverse aquatic ecosystem with several species of fish, reptiles, and amphibians.

Cheow Lan Lake, located within Khao Sok National Park, is another prominent attraction. The lake, formed by the construction of a dam, stretches for 165 square kilometers (64 square miles) and is surrounded by towering limestone cliffs and dense forests. The crystal-clear waters of the lake are perfect for swimming, kayaking, and exploring the numerous limestone karsts and hidden caves.

Visitors to Khao Sok National Park can engage in a range of activities, including jungle trekking, wildlife spotting, bird watching, canoeing, bamboo rafting, and night safaris. The park offers a variety of trails, ranging from easy walks to challenging hikes, allowing visitors to explore its pristine beauty at their own pace.

To preserve the delicate ecosystem, accommodations within the park are limited, with most visitors staying in nearby lodges and resorts. These establishments offer a range of accommodations, from basic bungalows to luxury tents, providing visitors with a comfortable and immersive nature experience.

In conclusion, Khao Sok National Park is a true ecological paradise, teeming with unparalleled biodiversity and natural beauty. Whether you are an adventure seeker, a nature enthusiast, or someone who appreciates the wonders of the natural world, a visit to Khao Sok is an unforgettable experience that allows you to immerse yourself in the splendor of Thailand's remarkable rainforest ecosystem.

## Doi Inthanon

 is the highest mountain in Thailand, located in the northern part of the country near Chiang Mai. It is a popular destination for nature lovers and outdoor enthusiasts due to its stunning peaks, scenic trails, and rich biodiversity.

The mountain is part of Doi Inthanon National Park, which covers an area of 482 square kilometers (186 square miles). The park is named after King Inthawichayanon, the last king of Chiang Mai, and was established in 1972 to protect the natural beauty and unique ecosystems of the area.

One of the main attractions of Doi Inthanon is its magnificent peaks. The summit, often shrouded in mist, reaches an elevation of 2,565 meters (8,415 feet) above sea level, offering breathtaking panoramic views of the surrounding valleys and mountains. Many visitors make the journey to the summit to witness the sunrise or sunset, which is a truly awe-inspiring experience.

The national park features a network of well-maintained trails, allowing visitors to explore the diverse landscapes and ecosystems of Doi Inthanon. There are several hiking trails of varying lengths and difficulty levels, catering to different preferences and fitness levels. These trails lead through lush forests, past cascading waterfalls, and to scenic viewpoints, providing an immersive and rewarding hiking experience.

The flora and fauna of Doi Inthanon are also exceptional. The mountain is covered in evergreen and deciduous forests, harboring a wide range of plant species, including orchids, rhododendrons, and mosses. The park is home to an abundance of bird species, making it a haven for birdwatchers. Species such as the Green-tailed Sunbird, White-browed Shortwing, and Ashy-throated Warbler can be spotted here. Other wildlife that can be found in the park includes macaques, gibbons, deer, and various reptiles and amphibians.

In addition to hiking, Doi Inthanon offers other activities for visitors to enjoy. The park has several picturesque waterfalls, such as Wachirathan and Mae Klang, where you can relax and take in the natural beauty. There are also opportunities for camping, picnicking, and visiting the nearby hill tribe villages to learn about the local culture and way of life.

It is worth noting that Doi Inthanon National Park is a protected area, and certain regulations are in place to ensure the preservation of its natural resources. Visitors are advised to follow the park rules, respect the environment, and engage in responsible tourism practices.

In summary, Doi Inthanon offers a captivating natural retreat in northern Thailand, with its majestic peaks, scenic trails, and diverse ecosystems. Whether you're a hiker, a nature enthusiast, or someone seeking tranquility amidst stunning landscapes, Doi Inthanon and its national park are a must-visit destination that showcases the remarkable beauty of Thailand's northern region.

# Erawan Falls

is indeed a beautiful natural attraction located in Kanchanaburi province, Thailand. It is known for its emerald-colored cascades and is a popular destination for nature lovers and outdoor enthusiasts.

**Here's some information about Erawan Falls:**
Location: Erawan Falls is situated in the Erawan National Park, approximately 65 kilometers (40 miles) northwest of Kanchanaburi town. The falls are nestled in the dense forests of the Tenasserim Hills.

Scenic Beauty: The falls consist of seven tiers, each with its own unique charm. The tiers are named after the seven-headed mythical serpent from Hindu mythology, Erawan. The emerald-green water and limestone formations create a picturesque setting. Visitors can swim in the pools formed by the cascades, making it a refreshing experience.

Hiking and Trekking: To reach the higher tiers of the falls, visitors can embark on a hiking trail that winds through the national park. The trail is well-maintained and passes through lush tropical forests, offering glimpses of various flora and fauna along the way. The trek can be moderately challenging, particularly for the upper tiers, but the effort is rewarded with breathtaking views and secluded swimming spots.

Wildlife: Erawan National Park is home to diverse wildlife, including macaques, gibbons, birds, butterflies, and various reptiles. Exploring the park allows visitors to appreciate the natural biodiversity of the region.

Facilities: The national park provides facilities such as restrooms, picnic areas, and food stalls near the entrance. However, it is advisable to bring your own food and water for the hike, especially if you plan to explore the higher tiers.

Entrance Fees: As of my knowledge cutoff in September 2021, there was an entrance fee for both Thai and foreign visitors. The fee for foreigners was higher compared to Thai nationals. However, keep in mind that policies and fees might change over time, so it is recommended to check the latest information before visiting.

Conservation: Erawan Falls and the surrounding area are protected under the Erawan National Park to preserve its natural beauty and ecological significance. Visitors are encouraged to follow park rules, including not littering and respecting the flora and fauna.

Overall, Erawan Falls is a stunning natural attraction in Kanchanaburi, Thailand, offering a tranquil escape into nature. Its emerald cascades, hiking trails, and abundant wildlife make it a popular destination for both locals and tourists alike.

## Thai cuisine

is renowned worldwide for its bold flavors, aromatic herbs, and vibrant colors. From the bustling streets of Bangkok to the high-end restaurants, Thai food offers a diverse range of dishes that cater to all tastes and preferences. Let's explore the fascinating world of Thai cuisine, from its humble street food delights to its refined offerings in fine dining establishments.

1. Street Food Delights:

Thai street food is a quintessential part of the local culinary experience. It's characterized by its affordability, quick preparation, and mouthwatering flavors. Whether you're strolling through the night markets or exploring the busy streets of Thailand, you'll find an array of delicious street food options such as:

- Pad Thai: This stir-fried rice noodle dish is a Thai street food classic. It typically includes shrimp, tofu, bean sprouts, eggs, and crushed peanuts, all flavored with tamarind sauce, fish sauce, and lime.

- Som Tam: Also known as green papaya salad, som tam combines shredded unripe papaya, tomatoes, green beans, peanuts, and chili peppers. The mixture is pounded together in a mortar and pestle, creating a delightful balance of sweet, sour, and spicy flavors.

- Satay: Skewered and grilled meat, usually chicken or pork, served with a peanut dipping sauce. Satay is a popular street food snack loved for its tender meat and flavorful marinades.

- Black tea, condensed milk, and ice are combined to make Thai Iced Tea, a cooling drink.. It has a distinct orange color and a sweet, creamy taste that complements the spicy flavors of Thai cuisine.

2. Regional Specialties:
Thai cuisine is not only diverse in terms of flavors but also varies regionally. Each region has its own specialties influenced by local ingredients and cooking styles. Here are a few examples:

- Northern Cuisine: Known for its hearty and robust flavors, northern Thai cuisine features dishes like Khao Soi, a coconut curry noodle soup, and Sai Oua, a flavorful northern Thai sausage.

- Northeastern Cuisine (Isan): Isan cuisine is heavily influenced by neighboring Laos and is known for its spicy and tangy dishes. Som Tam (papaya salad) and Larb (minced meat salad) are prominent dishes from this region.

- Southern Cuisine: Southern Thai cuisine is famous for its bold and fiery flavors. Dishes like Gaeng Tai Pla (southern Thai fish curry) and Massaman Curry (a rich and aromatic curry with Muslim influence) are popular examples.

3. Fine Dining Experience:
Thai cuisine has also made its mark in the realm of fine dining, offering a sophisticated and refined experience for food enthusiasts. Upscale Thai restaurants focus on artful presentation, innovative techniques, and premium ingredients to create a fusion of traditional Thai flavors with contemporary twists. These establishments often offer an extensive menu featuring dishes like:

- Tom Yum Goong: A hot and sour soup with shrimp, lemongrass, galangal, kaffir lime leaves, and other aromatic herbs. It showcases the harmonious balance of flavors that Thai cuisine is known for.

- Pla Neung Manao: Steamed fish with lime sauce, showcasing the delicate flavors of fresh fish paired with tangy and aromatic ingredients.

- Gaeng Keow Wan Gai: Also known as green curry chicken, this creamy and spicy curry is made with green chili paste, coconut milk, and a variety of herbs and vegetables.

- Mango Sticky Rice: A popular Thai dessert made with glutinous rice, fresh mango slices, and sweet coconut milk. It's a delightful combination of textures and flavors.

Whether you indulge in street food or opt for a fine dining experience, Thai cuisine offers a culinary journey that tantalizes the taste buds and showcases the rich cultural heritage of Thailand. Each bite is an explosion of flavors, combining sweet, spicy, sour, and savory elements in perfect harmony. Thai cuisine also emphasizes the use of fresh ingredients, aromatic herbs, and intricate spice blends, resulting in dishes that are both visually appealing and incredibly delicious.

Moreover, Thai food is deeply rooted in the country's cultural traditions and customs. It reflects the influence of neighboring countries such as China, India, and Malaysia, as well as indigenous culinary practices. Thai meals are often communal, with shared dishes placed in the center of the table, fostering a sense of togetherness and conviviality.

Furthermore, Thai cuisine places a strong emphasis on balancing flavors and textures. The combination of contrasting tastes, such as the spiciness of chili peppers, the tanginess of lime, the sweetness of palm sugar, and the saltiness of fish sauce, creates a symphony of sensations that truly delights the palate.

Whether you're savoring a humble street-side Pad Thai or indulging in an intricately prepared fine dining dish, Thai cuisine offers a remarkable culinary experience. Its ability to blend tradition with innovation, street food with fine dining, and flavors with cultural heritage makes Thai cuisine a cherished treasure in the culinary world.

## Thai massage

Thai yoga massage, sometimes called Nuad Thai or Thai massage, is a conventional medical technique that has its roots in Thailand.. It is a therapeutic technique that combines acupressure, stretching, and assisted yoga postures to promote relaxation, alleviate muscle tension, and restore balance in the body. Thai massage is deeply rooted in Thai culture and wellness traditions. Let's delve into the key aspects of Thai massage and its connection to overall wellness.

## 1. Origins and Philosophy:

Thai massage has its roots in ancient Indian Ayurvedic medicine, Buddhist practices, and traditional Chinese medicine. It is believed to have been developed by Jivaka Kumarabhacca, a physician to the Buddha, over 2,500 years ago. The practice incorporates the concept of energy lines, known as Sen lines, which are similar to the meridians in traditional Chinese medicine. According to Thai tradition, the body is a network of energy pathways through which life force energy, called "lom," flows. Thai massage aims to clear blockages along these energy lines and restore the balance of energy in the body.

## 2. Techniques and Benefits:

Thai massage involves a combination of techniques performed on a mat or padded floor, with the recipient wearing loose and comfortable clothing. The practitioner uses their hands, thumbs, elbows, knees, and feet to apply pressure to specific points along the Sen lines and gently stretch the body into yoga-like postures.

The advantages of Thai massage are various and incorporate:

- Relaxation and stress relief: Thai massage promotes deep relaxation, reduces stress, and calms the mind, allowing the recipient to experience a sense of tranquility and well-being.

- Improved flexibility and range of motion: The stretching and yoga-like movements involved in Thai massage help improve flexibility, increase joint mobility, and release muscle tension, making it beneficial for athletes and individuals with sedentary lifestyles alike.

- Enhanced energy flow: Thai massage is believed to unblock energy pathways, stimulate the flow of energy, and restore the balance of lom throughout the body, promoting vitality and overall wellness.

- Pain relief and muscle relaxation: The acupressure techniques used in Thai massage can help alleviate muscle and joint pain, reduce muscle tension, and improve circulation.

- Improved posture and body alignment: Thai massage incorporates gentle stretches and postural adjustments, which can help correct imbalances, improve posture, and promote better body alignment.

3. Traditional Thai Medicine and Herbal Remedies:
Thai massage is closely associated with traditional Thai medicine, which encompasses various holistic healing practices, including herbal remedies, dietary recommendations, and spiritual rituals. Traditional Thai medicine views the body as a whole, interconnected system, and seeks to restore balance and harmony in the body, mind, and spirit.

Herbal remedies play an integral role in Thai wellness traditions. Many Thai massage sessions incorporate the use of herbal compresses, known as Luk Pra Kob. These compresses contain a blend of therapeutic herbs and are steamed and applied to the body during the massage. The warmth and herbal properties enhance the therapeutic benefits of the massage, promoting relaxation, relieving pain, and improving overall well-being.

Thai massage and wellness traditions are deeply intertwined, reflecting the holistic approach to health and well-being in Thai culture. The practice offers not only physical benefits but also supports mental and emotional well-being, making it a popular choice for those seeking relaxation, rejuvenation, and a deeper connection to their bodies and inner selves.

## Loy Krathong and Songkran: Thailand's Colourful Festivals

Thailand is known for its vibrant and colourful festivals, two of the most famous being Loy Krathong and Songkran. These festivals hold great cultural and religious significance and attract both locals and tourists from around the world. Let's explore the unique traditions and joyful celebrations of Loy Krathong and Songkran.

1. Loy Krathong:
Loy Krathong, also known as the Festival of Lights, takes place on the full moon night of the twelfth lunar month, usually in November. The festival is celebrated by releasing krathongs, small lotus-shaped floats, onto rivers, canals, and other bodies of water. The krathongs are made from banana leaves, adorned with flowers, candles, and incense sticks. People place their wishes and prayers onto the krathongs before setting them afloat.

The festival signifies letting go of negativity, expressing gratitude, and paying respects to the water goddess, Phra Mae Khongkha. As the krathongs drift away, the candlelit waters create a mesmerizing sight, and the festival is filled with music, dancing, and fireworks. Loy Krathong is celebrated nationwide, but particularly in cities like Bangkok, Chiang Mai, and Sukhothai.

2. Songkran:
Songkran, the Thai New Year festival, is one of the most exhilarating and widely celebrated events in Thailand. It occurs from April 13th to 15th each year and marks the transition from the old year to the new year. Songkran is famous for its water fights, symbolizing the cleansing of sins and the fresh start that comes with the New Year.

During Songkran, people take to the streets armed with water guns, buckets, and hoses, playfully dousing each other with water. It's a joyous celebration of laughter, camaraderie, and relief from the summer heat. Temples play an important role during Songkran, where people offer prayers, make merit, and pour water over Buddha statues and the hands of revered elders as a sign of respect and blessings.

Songkran is celebrated throughout Thailand, with particularly lively festivities in cities like Bangkok, Chiang Mai, and Pattaya. Tourists flock to these destinations to partake in the festivities and experience the exuberant water fights.

Both Loy Krathong and Songkran are deeply rooted in Thai traditions, customs, and beliefs. They showcase the Thai people's strong connection to nature, spirituality, and community. These festivals are not only an opportunity to celebrate and have fun but also to reflect on the past, express gratitude, and welcome new beginnings. They provide a unique insight into Thai culture and are an unforgettable experience for both locals and visitors.

## Amphawa

is a charming town located about 90 kilometers southwest of Bangkok, and it offers a delightful escape from the bustling city. Known for its floating markets and riverside charm, Amphawa is a hidden gem that provides a unique and authentic Thai experience. Let's explore the highlights of this off-the-beaten-path destination.

1. Amphawa Floating Market:
One of the main attractions in Amphawa is its floating market, which takes place along the canals of the Mae Klong River. Unlike the more touristy floating markets in Bangkok, the Amphawa Floating Market retains its local charm and authenticity. Here, you can witness local vendors selling a variety of fresh produce, seafood, snacks, and traditional Thai dishes from their boats. It's a vibrant and lively scene, and exploring the market by boat or strolling along the canal-side walkways is a must-do experience.

2. Firefly Boat Tour:
One of the highlights of visiting Amphawa is the opportunity to witness the enchanting spectacle of fireflies illuminating the night sky. You can take a boat tour along the canals at dusk, where you'll be surrounded by the mesmerizing glow of

fireflies. It's a magical experience that showcases the natural beauty of the area.

3. Wat Bang Kung:

Wat Bang Kung is a historic temple located in Amphawa and is known for its unique architecture and fascinating history. The temple is situated within the roots of a banyan tree, creating a remarkable and picturesque sight. It has a rich cultural and historical significance, as it was once a hiding place for Thai warriors during battles with the Burmese army.

4. Local Homestays and Riverside Accommodations:

To fully immerse yourself in the local way of life, consider staying at one of the homestays or riverside accommodations available in Amphawa. These accommodations offer a glimpse into the traditional Thai lifestyle, allowing you to interact with friendly locals, savor home-cooked Thai meals, and experience the tranquility of riverside living.

5. Temple-Hopping and Cycling:

Amphawa is surrounded by lush countryside and picturesque temples. Renting a bicycle and exploring the area is a fantastic way to uncover hidden gems and encounter local life. You can visit temples such as Wat Bang Khae Noi and Wat Bang Khae Yai, which are off the beaten path and offer a serene and peaceful atmosphere.

Amphawa provides a unique and authentic Thai experience, away from the tourist crowds. It's a place where you can immerse yourself in the local way of life, witness the charm of floating markets, discover hidden temples, and connect with nature. If you're seeking a more off-the-beaten-path adventure in Thailand, Amphawa is a destination that should not be missed.

# Ko Tao

meaning "Turtle Island" in Thai, is a small island located in the Gulf of Thailand. Despite its size, Ko Tao is renowned for its serene beauty, crystal-clear waters, and vibrant marine life. It has gained popularity as a diving destination, offering incredible diving adventures for both beginners and experienced divers. Let's explore what makes Ko Tao a haven for nature lovers and diving enthusiasts.

1. Diving and Snorkeling:
Ko Tao is often referred to as one of the best diving spots in the world, thanks to its stunning coral reefs, diverse marine ecosystems, and excellent visibility. The island boasts a plethora of dive sites suitable for all levels of experience. Whether you're a novice looking to get certified or an advanced diver seeking thrilling underwater encounters, Ko Tao has something for everyone.

Popular dive sites around Ko Tao include Chumphon Pinnacle, Ṣail Rock, Shark Island, and Mango Bay. These sites offer opportunities to spot a wide variety of marine life, including colorful coral reefs, tropical fish, sea turtles, rays, and even whale sharks if you're lucky. Snorkeling is also a fantastic way to explore the vibrant underwater world around the island, with easily accessible snorkeling spots near the shore.

2. Beaches and Island Hopping:
Ko Tao is blessed with picturesque beaches and secluded coves, making it an ideal destination for beach lovers. Sairee Beach is the most popular beach on the island, offering powdery white sand, clear turquoise waters, and a lively atmosphere with beachfront bars and restaurants. Other beautiful beaches worth exploring include Ao Tanote, Sai Nuan Beach, and Shark Bay.

For those looking to venture beyond Ko Tao, the island serves as a gateway to nearby islands, including Ko Nang Yuan, a stunning island with a triple-pronged sandbar. Island hopping tours allow you to visit these pristine islands, relax on secluded beaches, and snorkel in untouched waters.

3. Viewpoints and Hiking:
Ko Tao is not just about the underwater wonders—it also boasts breathtaking viewpoints and opportunities for hiking and exploration. One popular viewpoint is the John-Suwan Viewpoint, which offers panoramic vistas of the island and its surrounding turquoise waters. The challenging hike to Two Views Rock is rewarded with stunning vistas of both the east and west sides of Ko Tao.

4. Vibrant Nightlife and Culinary Delights:
Despite its serene ambiance, Ko Tao has a lively nightlife scene, particularly around Sairee Beach. The beach bars come alive in the evenings with live music, fire shows, and social gatherings. You can enjoy beachside dining, sample delicious Thai cuisine, and indulge in fresh seafood from local restaurants.

Ko Tao is truly a paradise for nature enthusiasts and diving aficionados. Its serene beauty, rich marine life, stunning beaches, and adventurous activities make it an unforgettable destination. Whether you're seeking underwater exploration, relaxation on pristine beaches, or immersing yourself in the island's vibrant atmosphere, Ko Tao offers a perfect blend of tranquility and adventure.

## Trang

is a province located in southern Thailand, known for its untouched beaches, idyllic islands, and stunning marine national parks. If you're looking for a destination off the beaten path, Trang offers a serene and unspoiled paradise for beach lovers and nature enthusiasts. Let's explore the highlights of Trang's pristine beaches and marine national parks.

1. Trang Islands:
Trang is home to a collection of beautiful islands that offer a tranquil escape from the crowds. The

most famous islands include Koh Ngai, Koh Kradan, and Koh Mook. These islands boast powdery white sand beaches, crystal-clear turquoise waters, and vibrant coral reefs. You can relax on secluded beaches, snorkel in the colorful underwater world, and indulge in the serenity of island life.

Koh Libong is another noteworthy island in Trang known for its wildlife. It's home to the endangered dugong, a marine mammal also known as the "sea cow." You can take a boat tour around the island and have the chance to spot these gentle creatures in their natural habitat.

2. Hat Chao Mai National Park:
Hat Chao Mai National Park is a protected area encompassing pristine beaches, mangrove forests, and diverse marine ecosystems. The park is home to several beaches, including Hat Chang Lang and Hat San Beach, where you can relax and enjoy the untouched beauty of nature. Exploring the mangrove forests by boat or kayak is a popular activity, offering an opportunity to

observe the unique flora and fauna that thrive in these coastal habitats.

### 3. Mu Ko Phetra National Park:
Mu Ko Phetra National Park is another gem in Trang province, comprising a group of islands, coral reefs, and coastal forests. The park is known for its stunning beaches, such as Hat Yao and Hat Chao Mai, which are perfect for swimming, sunbathing, and picnicking.

### 4. Snorkeling and Diving:
Trang's marine national parks offer exceptional opportunities for snorkeling and diving. The clear waters and diverse marine life make it a paradise for underwater exploration. You can discover vibrant coral reefs teeming with colorful fish, sea turtles, and other fascinating marine species. Diving and snorkeling trips can be arranged from Trang town or through resorts on the islands, allowing you to immerse yourself in the beauty of the underwater world.

### 5. Emerald Cave (Tham Morakot):

Located on Koh Mook, the Emerald Cave is a hidden gem that shouldn't be missed. Accessible only by swimming through a dark tunnel, you'll emerge into a mesmerizing emerald-colored lagoon surrounded by towering cliffs. The secluded and mystical atmosphere of the cave and lagoon make it an unforgettable experience.

Trang's untouched beaches and marine national parks offer a serene and natural escape from the tourist crowds. Whether you're seeking relaxation on pristine beaches, snorkeling in vibrant coral reefs, or exploring the beauty of coastal forests, Trang provides a paradise for those in search of unspoiled natural beauty.

# Safety tips

When traveling to Thailand, it's important to prioritize your safety to ensure a smooth and enjoyable trip. Here are some safety tips to keep in mind:

1. Research and Stay Informed: Before your trip, research the destination thoroughly. Stay updated on travel advisories, local laws, customs, and potential risks. The website of your country's embassy or consulate in Thailand is a valuable resource for travel information.

2. Carry Important Documents Safely: Keep your passport, identification, and other important documents secure. Consider making digital copies and storing them in a secure online location for backup.

3. Stay Health-conscious: Stay hydrated, use sunscreen, and protect yourself from mosquito bites, particularly in areas where mosquito-borne diseases like dengue fever are prevalent. Carry

necessary medications and consult a healthcare professional about vaccinations and health precautions before traveling.

4. Stay Aware of Your Surroundings: Be aware of your surroundings at all times, especially in crowded areas or public transportation. Avoid displaying valuable items openly, and keep an eye on your belongings to prevent theft.

5. Transportation Safety: Choose reputable and licensed transportation options. Ensure that seat belts are available and use them when traveling by car or taxi. Exercise caution when using motorcycles or renting vehicles, and always wear helmets.

6. Street and Food Safety: While Thai street food is delicious, choose vendors that have high turnover and maintain cleanliness. Ensure that the food is freshly prepared and cooked thoroughly. Drink bottled water or use a water purifier.

7. Scams and Tourist Touts: Be cautious of scams and tourist touts, particularly in popular tourist areas. Be skeptical of unsolicited offers, overly friendly strangers, and deals that seem too good to be true. Use authorized tour operators and be cautious of booking through unverified sources.

8. Respect Local Customs and Laws: Familiarize yourself with Thai customs and laws to avoid any unintentional offenses or legal issues. Dress modestly when visiting temples or religious sites, and adhere to local customs and traditions.

9. Use Reliable Transportation Services: When using taxis or ride-sharing services, opt for reputable companies or those recommended by your hotel. Ensure that the driver uses the meter or agrees on a fare before starting the journey.

10. Trust Your Instincts: If a situation feels uncomfortable or unsafe, trust your instincts and remove yourself from it. Seek assistance from authorities or hotel staff if needed.

Remember that safety precautions can vary depending on the specific location and circumstances. It's always a good idea to stay informed and adapt to local conditions while maintaining a sensible and cautious approach. By taking these safety tips into account, you can enjoy your time in Thailand with peace of mind.

# Transportation Options and Getting Around

When it comes to transportation options and getting around in Thailand, here are some practical tips and resources to help you navigate the country:

1. Domestic Flights: Thailand has a well-developed domestic flight network, making it convenient to travel between major cities and popular destinations. Airlines like Thai Airways,

Bangkok Airways, and low-cost carriers such as AirAsia and Nok Air offer domestic flights. Booking in advance or taking advantage of promotional fares can help you find affordable flights.

2. Trains: Thailand's railway system connects major cities and towns, offering a scenic and budget-friendly mode of transportation. The State Railway of Thailand operates both overnight sleeper trains and regular trains with various classes and amenities. Booking tickets in advance, especially for popular routes, is advisable. The official website of the State Railway of Thailand provides schedules, fares, and online booking options.

3. Buses: Buses are a common mode of transportation for both short and long distances in Thailand. There are different types of buses available, including standard buses, VIP buses with more comfort, and minivans. The quality and amenities vary depending on the type of bus and the company operating it. Tickets can be

purchased at bus terminals or through online platforms like 12Go Asia and BusOnlineTicket, which provide route options, schedules, and online booking services.

4. Taxis and Ride-Sharing: Taxis are widely available in major cities, and most use meters. It's a good practice to ensure the meter is turned on or negotiate a fare before starting the ride. Ride-sharing services like Grab are also available in Bangkok and other cities, providing a convenient and often more affordable alternative to traditional taxis. The Grab app can be downloaded and used for booking rides.

5. Local Transportation: Within cities, you'll find various modes of local transportation. Tuk-tuks, three-wheeled motorized vehicles, are common in tourist areas and can be a fun way to get around short distances, but always negotiate the fare before getting in. Motorcycle taxis are another option for short trips. Additionally, cities like Bangkok have efficient mass transit systems, including the BTS Skytrain and MRT

subway, which are convenient for navigating the city center.

6. Renting Motorbikes or Cars: If you have a valid international driving license, renting a motorbike or car can give you more flexibility and independence, especially in rural areas. However, it's important to familiarize yourself with local traffic laws and road conditions, exercise caution, and wear helmets when riding motorbikes. Rental agencies are available at airports, major cities, and tourist areas.

7. Language and Maps: While English is widely spoken in tourist areas, it's helpful to learn a few basic Thai phrases for communication. Google Maps is a reliable resource for navigating Thai cities and finding directions. Additionally, offline maps and translation apps can be useful when internet access is limited.

It's always advisable to plan your transportation in advance, especially during peak travel seasons, to secure seats and get the best fares.

Consider the distances and travel times between destinations, as well as any visa requirements or travel restrictions that may be in place. Taking these practical tips into account will help you have a smoother and more enjoyable experience exploring Thailand.

# Language Essentials and Useful Phrases

While English is widely spoken in tourist areas of Thailand, learning a few basic Thai phrases can greatly enhance your travel experience and show respect for the local culture. Here are some essential phrases and useful expressions to help you communicate:

1. Basic Greetings:
- Hello: Sawasdee (sa-wat-dee)
- Goodbye: Laa gòn (laa-gon)
- Thank you: Khop khun (kɔɔp kun)
- Yes: Chai (chai)
- No: Mai chai (mai chai)

2. Polite Expressions:
- Excuse me: Khor thot (kɔɔr thɔɔt)
- Sorry: Khor thot (kɔɔr thɔɔt)
- Please: Karuna (ka-roo-nah)
- May I...?: Khor pom/dichan... dai mai (kɔɔr pɔm/di-chan... dai mai)

3. Ordering Food:
- I would like...: Ao (item) krab/ka (ao... krɔɔb/kaa)
- Water: Nam (nam)
- Rice: Khao (khao)
- Spicy: Pet (pet)
- No spicy: Mai pet (mai pet)
- Delicious: Aroy (a-roy)

4. Directions:
- Where is...?: Yu ti nai...? (yoo tee nai...?)
- Left: Sai (sai)
- Right: Kwaa (kwaa)
- Straight ahead: Trong pai (trong pai)
- How much is it?: Tao rai (tao rai)

5. Numbers:

- One: Neung (neung)
- Two: Song (song)
- Three: Sam (sam)
- Four: See (see)
- Five: Ha (ha)
- Ten: Sip (sip)

6. Basic Conversation:
- What is your name?: Kun chue a-rai? (kun chuu-ay-rai?)
- My name is...: Pom/di-chan chue... (pɔm/di-chan chuu...)
- Where are you from?: Kun maa jaak bprateet nai? (kun maa jaak bprà-teet nai?)
- I don't understand: Mai kao jai (mai kao jai)
- Can you help me?: Chuay pom/di-chan dai mai? (chûuay pɔm/di-chan dai mai?)

Remember to use the polite particles "krab" (for males) or "ka" (for females) at the end of your sentences to show respect. The pronunciation guide in parentheses above should help you get the right intonation for each phrase.

Thai people appreciate the effort made by foreigners to speak their language, so even if your pronunciation isn't perfect, trying to use a few Thai phrases will likely bring a smile to their faces and help you connect on a deeper level during your travels in Thailand.

# Recommended Travel Apps and Websites

When planning your trip to Thailand, several travel apps and websites can be useful for finding information, making reservations, navigating, and discovering local recommendations. Here are some recommended travel apps and websites:

1. Google Maps: A reliable and widely used mapping app that provides detailed maps, directions, and transportation information. You can save offline maps for areas with limited internet connectivity.

2. Skyscanner or Kayak: These flight search engines allow you to compare prices, find the best deals on flights, and book tickets.

3. Agoda or Booking.com: Popular hotel booking platforms that offer a wide range of accommodations, from budget guesthouses to luxury resorts. They provide user reviews, photos, and competitive rates.

4. Airbnb: A platform that offers unique accommodations, such as private rooms, apartments, and houses, often providing a more local and immersive experience.

5. TripAdvisor: A comprehensive website and app that offers reviews, recommendations, and ratings for hotels, restaurants, attractions, and activities. It can help you plan your itinerary and find hidden gems.

6. Grab or Uber (if available): Ride-hailing apps that provide convenient and reliable transportation options, particularly in urban

areas like Bangkok. They offer both car and motorbike taxi services.

7. 12Go Asia: A booking platform that allows you to purchase bus, train, ferry, and flight tickets within Thailand and other Southeast Asian countries. It provides schedules, prices, and secure online booking options.

8. Thai National Parks Official Website: If you plan to visit national parks in Thailand, the official website provides information on park locations, entrance fees, accommodations, and activities.

9. Thai Chana App: Developed by the Thai government, this app provides COVID-19-related information, including tracking hotspots, checking-in at venues, and receiving alerts. It's useful for staying updated on health and safety measures during your trip.

10. Thai language learning apps: Apps like Duolingo, Memrise, or Learn Thai - Phrasebook

for Travel can help you learn basic Thai phrases and improve your language skills before and during your trip.

11. Google translator

These apps and websites can assist you in various aspects of your travel planning and exploration in Thailand, from finding the best flight and accommodation deals to discovering local attractions and navigating the country with ease. Always check the latest reviews, compare prices, and read the terms and conditions before making any bookings.

# Conclusion

Fond Farewell and Lasting Memories
As your journey through Thailand comes to an end, it's time to bid a fond farewell to this captivating country that has filled your days with vibrant experiences, delectable cuisine, cultural wonders, and breathtaking landscapes. From the

bustling streets of Bangkok to the serene beaches of Trang, Thailand has left an indelible mark on your heart and soul.

As you reflect on your adventures, take a moment to cherish the lasting memories you've created. The tantalizing aromas of street food delicacies, the tranquil moments spent on hidden beaches, the exhilaration of diving into vibrant underwater worlds, and the warmth of Thai hospitality—these are the treasures that will stay with you long after you've left the Land of Smiles.

Remember the enchanting traditions and festivals that painted the streets with colors and brought communities together. Relish the rejuvenation and relaxation experienced through traditional Thai massage and wellness practices, immersing yourself in the country's rich cultural heritage.

Whether you explored the bustling metropolis or ventured off the beaten path to discover hidden gems, Thailand has opened your eyes to a world of beauty, diversity, and endless possibilities. From the floating markets of Amphawa to the serene beauty of Ko Tao, each destination has added a unique chapter to your Thai adventure.

As you bid farewell, take with you the essence of Thailand—the warm smiles, the gracious hospitality, and the sense of community that pervades every corner of the country. Keep the memories alive, and perhaps one day, you'll find yourself drawn back to the enchanting charms of Thailand to create even more lasting moments.

Farewell, Thailand. Until we meet again, may your beauty and wonders continue to captivate the hearts of travelers from around the world.

Made in United States
Troutdale, OR
07/05/2023

10978230R00136